WHAT IS SECULAR HUMANISM?

What Is Secular Humanism?

Why Humanism Became Secular and
How It Is Changing Our World

James Hitchcock

RC BOOKS
P.O. Box 255
Harrison, NY 10528

ISBN 0-89283-163-4
Printed in the United States of America

Photo Credits. Historical Pictures Service, Inc., pp: 12, 45,
        51, 103
        Wide World Photos, pp: 16, 62, 92, 95, 149
        Religious News Service, pp: 29, 38, 42, 47, 65,
        73, 89, 112, 125, 128, 135, 143

Contents

ONE

What Is Secular Humanism?

IN RECENT YEARS, the term "secular humanism" has been bandied about more and more in the public arena. There are few terms about which there is more confusion and controversy. The very use of quotation marks, the custom in the press, implies that "secular humanism" is something which, although people talk about it, does not really exist. It is a kind of bogey man invented by certain hysterical individuals to discredit others with whom they happen to disagree. For example, *Newsweek* magazine, in its 1981 cover story on "the New Right," disposed of "secular humanism" in exactly this way.

But if secular humanism is a phantom, it is a remarkably solid one. Its existence is attested to, for example, by an organization called the American Humanist Association and its rather widely read journal, *The Humanist*. The movement was even given legal status by the U.S. Supreme Court in one of its landmark decisions (*Torcaso v. Watkins,* 1961).

Since many people consider the term *humanist* a mark of pride, and since increasing numbers also do not deny being secularists, why is it so hard to establish the existence of a secular humanist movement? Part of the answer is that secular humanism has in certain ways become a privileged and ubiquitous point of view, and it is in the interests of its adherents to deny their own existence, or rather to deny the cohesiveness and influence of their philosophy, in order not to provoke challenges. Further, the term *humanist* has itself led to some of the shadowed confusion, since it has at least four quite distinct meanings.

In the narrowest sense, a humanist is someone who is interested, often in a professional way, in those intellectual and academic disciplines called the humanities—so called because they deal with human nature in its fullness, the non-rational side of man as well as the rational. These have traditionally included literature, history, the fine arts, philosophy, and sometimes theology. Alexander Pope's dictum that "the proper study of mankind is man" is a watchword of the discipline. The humanities tend to be somewhat intuitive and do not make man an object of properly scientific scrutiny.

There is nothing at all pejorative in calling someone a humanist in this sense. Indeed there have been many outstanding Christian humanists, such as the late C.S. Lewis. Christianity has been blessed with large numbers of this kind of humanist throughout its history.

This first meaning of "humanist" is to a certain extent derivative of a second, broader meaning. One only studies the creations of the human mind and imagination because of a conviction that human beings have inherent dignity and that what they do can be noble and inspiring. This second kind of humanism distinguishes itself from rather opposite attitudes.

One is the kind of religion that completely abases man before deity, leaving him no shred of dignity or goodness. Man is almost a plaything of the gods, subject to their arbitrary whims. This is the religion of some cultures, but, though it has occasionally been the teaching of perverted forms of Christianity, it is not the religion of the Bible.

At the other extreme is anti-humanism in two major forms. One regards man as totally insignificant, a mere speck in a vast universe. At various times, mechanistic philosophies have proposed that man lacks any spiritual dimension and is merely a kind of advanced automaton. In recent times this anti-humanism has often predicted that man will be "replaced" by robots, computers, and other machines which will render him obsolete. The other form of anti-humanism dwells on all that is sordid, animalistic, and degraded in human existence, not to seek to elevate it but to proclaim in triumph, "See! Man has a high opinion of himself, but when you strip away the trappings, this is what he is."

Christians are, by definition, humanists in this second sense. They cannot acquiesce in a philosophy which denies the goodness of God's creation by degrading humanity. There is a God-given natural dignity to man which even the best of the pagans have recognized, and which Christians must affirm.

A third meaning of "humanist" is someone who expresses a special loyalty to man as distinct from nature.

From the time of Socrates (c. 400 B.C.), the Western tradition was increasingly humanistic, shifting its attention from the heavens and the earth to humanity itself. Beginning with the Scientific Revolution of the seventeenth century, the emphasis began to shift back toward nature again, as the most exciting discoveries seemed to be in nonhuman areas of reality. In recent years, this shift back to nature has been given a strong impetus by the so-called environmentalist movement—the desire to protect forests, streams, oceans, wild animals, etc., from pollution or destruction by human use. To a degree this environmental concern must be regarded as itself humanistic, since man cannot live properly if he wantonly destroys nature. Carried to an extreme, however, it becomes anti-humanistic. Some environmentalists would gladly see mankind fall back to a rather primitive level of existence in order to protect nature. Some argue that animals have rights equal to human beings, and that it is no less immoral to kill a bear than a person. An increasing number of environmentalists would drastically restrict the birth of human beings, by coercion if necessary, in order to protect nature.

In this conflict Christians must surely all be humanists. They must assert that man is indeed superior to nature and has dominion over it. They cannot acquiesce in what sometimes approaches a neo-paganism that worships nature. Significantly, extreme environmentalists are seldom believing Christians. They often express admiration for Native American religions, for example, and they repudiate the biblical understanding of man as the steward of creation. Christians are responsible humanists who are environmentalists precisely because they recognize the heavy responsibility laid on their shoulders by this stewardship. They consider man a unique creation of God.

If the third kind of humanism sets man apart from nature, the fourth sets man apart from God. This is where the trouble begins.

Groups like the American Humanist Association are not humanists just in the sense that they have an interest in the humanities or that they value man over nature (indeed some self-proclaimed humanists are in fact extreme environmentalists). In their self-definition, God does not exist, and it is a destructive illusion to believe in him. They promote a way of life that systematically excludes God and all religion in the traditional sense. Man, for better or for worse, is on his own in the universe. He marks the highest point to which nature has yet evolved, and he must rely entirely on his own resources.

Obviously Christians, Jews, Moslems, and adherents of most other religions of the world cannot possibly be humanists in this sense.

To call someone a humanist is usually a term of honor. It is when the adjective "secular" is added that the trouble begins. "Secular humanism" is a perfectly just and accurate description of the third kind of humanism, and it helps avoid terminological confusion. However, Secular Humanists like to avoid the adjective because, as already suggested, they trade on this terminological confusion. Since humanist is a term of praise, they like to smuggle in their own particular kind under its wide mantle.

But the adjective "secular" is both just and necessary. It comes from the Latin "saeculum," which means "time" or "age" (as in the Latin prayer of the Catholic Church "in saecula saeculorum"—literally, "through all ages of ages," commonly translated "forever and ever").

To call someone secular means that he is completely time-bound, totally a child of his age, a creature of history, with no vision of eternity. Unable to see anything in the perspective of eternity, he cannot believe that God exists or acts in human affairs. Moral standards, for example, tend to be merely those commonly accepted by the society in which he lives, and he believes that everything changes, so that there are no enduring or permanent values.

In 1933 the American Humanist Association issued its *Humanist Manifesto,* a creed for the movement. The manifesto identified Humanism as "religious" but deplored "the identification of the word *religion* with doctrines and methods which have lost their significance and which are powerless to solve the problem of human living in the Twentieth Century." Among the major tenets of its own "religious humanism" were:

Religious humanists regard the universe as self-existing and not created.

Humanism asserts that the nature of the universe depicted by modern science makes unacceptable any supernatural or cosmic guarantees of human values.

Religious humanism considers the complete realization of human personality to be the end of man's life and seeks its development and fulfillment in the here and now.

In the place of the old attitudes involved in worship and prayer the humanist finds his religious emotions expressed in a heightened sense of personal life and in a cooperative effort to promote social well-being.

Man is at last becoming aware that he alone is responsible for the realization of the world of his dreams, that he has within himself the power for its achievement.[1]

The authors of this manifesto did not deny the existence of God. By their silence they seemed to leave it open, at least as a possibility. But the whole thrust of the document was to deny that belief in God could, or ought to, have any practical effect. Whether or not God is thought to exist, man must live as if he did not exist. Thus, Secular Humanism is not strictly atheism,

John Dewey (1859-1952) was probably the most influential American philosopher, especially in the field of education. One of Dewey's principal claims was that education should be a preparation for democratic living, as defined in a supposedly "neutral," but in fact secular, way. The main author of the first *Humanist Manifesto,* Dewey once wrote: "It is the business of those who do not believe that religion is a monopoly or a protected industry to contend, in the interest of both education and religion, for keeping the schools free from what they must regard as a false bias."

although it is likely that most Humanists are atheists. It is possible to believe in God abstractly, so long as one does not act as though He exists.

Another major tenet of modern Humanism articulated in this document was that moral values could have no "supernatural or cosmic guarantees." This requires the rejection of any specifically religious morality. The only recognized morality is that which emerges from continuous human experience. There are no moral absolutes.

The seemingly benign phrase "the complete realization of the human personality," easily overlooked amidst the rhetoric of the document, would prove to have great significance over the next fifty years. It would lie at the root of the far-reaching moral and social revolution wrought in Western culture after 1960.

This *Humanist Manifesto* did not attract much attention at the time of its proclamation. The original signers numbered only thirty-four. Most of them were people now forgotten, but a few stand out: the noted historian Harry Elmer Barnes; the influential philosopher John Herman Randall; Lester Mondale, whose half-brother would become vice-president of the United States in 1977. Towering above all others, however, was the man reputed to be the principal author of the document—the philosopher John Dewey. A longtime professor at Columbia University, Dewey was probably the most influential philosopher in American history. No one had more influence over the theory and practice of public education in the United States in the twentieth century. The manifesto certainly represented Dewey's personal beliefs, and through it he was able to disseminate them widely and strategically.

Forty years later, a second *Humanist Manifesto* was issued, an updating of the first. Among its major tenets were:

... traditional dogmatic or authoritarian religions that place revelation, God, ritual, or creed above human need or experience do a disservice to the human species.
... we can discover no divine purpose or providence for the human species. While there is much that we do not know,

humans are responsible for what we are or will become. No deity will save us; we must save ourselves.

We affirm that moral values derive their source from human experience. Ethics is *autonomous* and *situational*, needing no theological or ideological sanction. In the area of sexuality, we believe that intolerant attitudes, often cultivated by orthodox religions and puritanical cultures, unduly repress sexual conduct. The right to birth control, abortion, and divorce should be recognized.[2]

There was nothing substantially new in *Humanist Manifesto II*. Considerably longer than the first version, it was also bolder in its sallies against traditional religion. The 1933 document had been prudently silent on the subject of sex, which the framers of the 1973 document obviously recognized as a key point of conflict with religious believers.

The list of signers for the second manifesto was considerably longer than for the first, indicating that Humanism had become more respectable in the intervening forty years. It included:

—influential philosophers Brand Blanshard, Antony Flew, Sidney Hook, John Herman Randall, Jr., and Sir Alfred Ayer;
—authors Isaac Asimov and John Ciardi;
—Paul Blanshard, for many years the most prominent anti-Catholic writer in the United States;
—prominent scientists Francis Crick, Andrei Sakharov, Zhores Medvedev, and Herbert Muller (Sakharov and Medvedev are Soviet dissidents);
—Edd Doerr, director of the organization Americans United For Separation of Church and State (formerly Protestants and Other Americans United), which played a major role in the secularizing of public education in the United States afterWorld War II;
—leading "sexologists" Albert Ellis, Lester A. Kirkendall, and Sol Gordon;

—influential psychologists H.J. Eysenck and B.F. Skinner;
—Allen F. Guttmacher, president of the Planned Parenthood Federation of America;
—Lawrence Lader, chairman of the National Association for the Repeal of Abortion Laws;
—Joseph Fletcher, an Episcopal clergyman and the leading proponent of "situation ethics" in the United States;
—Betty Friedan, founder of the National Organization of Women;
—Gunnar Myrdal, a Swedish economist with worldwide influence;
—A. Philip Randolph, a long-time leader in both the labor and civil-rights movements in the United States.

The importance of the *Humanist Manifestoes* has sometimes been dismissed on the grounds that the association which issued them has only a few thousand members. But, as the second list of signers particularly shows, numbers are not the crucial test of importance. Those who subscribe to this creed are strategically placed in highly sensitive areas of modern life. In addition to tremendous personal and intellectual influence, they have the means to influence public opinion to a degree far in excess of their numerical strength.

Modern Humanists have been highly effective propagandists. Many people imbibe their message without realizing that it is the creed of a particular movement. They have cleverly preempted the vocabulary of freedom: "All we want is the right to believe our own creed, as we concede to you the right to believe yours. Let us do away with all forms of intolerance." Yet in practice, as *Humanist Manifesto II* particularly shows, Humanists are intolerant of religious belief. Paul Kurtz, editor of *The Humanist* magazine, says, "Humanism cannot in any fair sense of the word apply to one who still believes in God as the source and creator of the universe. Christian Humanism would be possible only for those who are willing to admit that they are atheistic Humanists. It surely does not apply to God-intoxicated

Betty Friedan, through her book *The Feminine Mystique,* was one of the founders of the feminist movement. She was also a signer of the second *Humanist Manifesto.* One of her few explicit statements about religion is: "Women of orthodox Catholic or Jewish origin do not easily break through the housewife image; it is enshrined in the canons of their religion, in the assumptions of their own and their husbands' childhoods, and in their church's dogmatic definitions of marriage and motherhood." Although there are religious feminists, Betty Friedan exemplifies the practice whereby feminists and other political groups judge religion in the light of their own beliefs and demand that the churches conform to them.

believers." He goes on to say that Humanism is "squarely in opposition" to movements which seek "to impose an orthodoxy of belief or morality."[3]

Humanism is hardly the benign, tolerant force it pretends to be. Indeed, it is highly intolerant. It has a keen sense of being locked into a continuous philosophical and social struggle with religious belief, in which the ultimate stakes are nothing less than the moral foundations of society.

Until the 1960s, the term Secular Humanism was scarcely heard in public discourse. Most people would probably not even have known what it meant. The beliefs set forth in *Humanist Manifesto I* were probably repugnant to most Americans, who considered themselves a God-fearing people. The greater boldness of *Humanist Manifesto II* shows that sometime after 1960 the climate of public opinion began to change. In that sense, Secular Humanism can be said to be a recent invention, but its roots also go far back in time. It represents the climax of certain cultural forces which have been operative for over two centuries. It involves certain very subtle but crucial ideas about the nature of humanity. Its pedigree is lengthy, with distinguished names on many branches of its family tree.

TWO

The Road to Modernity

WESTERN CIVILIZATION is chiefly the product of a dynamic mixture of two elements—the Judaeo-Christian religious tradition and the tradition of rational investigation and artistic creativity coming down from the Greeks. Most developments of the past 2500 years can be seen as offshoots of one or the other.

The two are, obviously, not mutually exclusive. Although the Jews, out of principle, did not produce religious art, they did build a splendid temple, and the Old Testament contains writing that is recognized as artistically powerful even by nonbelievers.

But the Hebrews were not very interested in art as such and probably did not care whether the Scripture was artistically powerful. Their intellectual inquiry was in the Scripture itself. They had little that could be called philosophy or science, and, unlike the Babylonians and the Egyptians, did not deeply pursue the study of mathematics.

The Greeks believed in the supernatural. If anything, their problem was too many gods. Their polytheism, in conjunction with a strong sense that an inexorable fate ruled the universe, produced a rather weak concept of divinity. Greek mythology presented a picture of the gods which was not very edifying (they often acted churlishly and even immorally) and ultimately not very convincing.

The Old Testament is the story of a people who lived continually in the presence of an all-powerful, all-wise, all-just,

all-loving God. There are certain humanist themes in the
Jewish Scriptures ("What is man that Thou art mindful of him?
Thou hast made him a little lower than the angels and hast
clothed him with glory and honor" [Ps 8:4-5]), but on the whole
the Israelites were exhorted to depend utterly on God. When
they relied on themselves they went astray. Among the Greeks,
by contrast, the religious sense got weaker and weaker. Of
necessity, unable ultimately to rely on their gods, the Greeks
pursued wisdom through their own resources. They virtually
invented philosophy and science and perfected mathematics,
medicine, drama, poetry, sculpture, architecture, and the study
of history.

The Greeks were preeminently a humanistic people in that
they took immense pride in humanity and its achievements.
They enjoyed the interplay of philosophical dialogue, pondered
the conundrums of human existence as portrayed on the stage,
delved into the secrets of nature, and celebrated all the glories of
humanity. (The famous Greek nude statues were intended to
display the perfection both of the human form as well as the
artist's skill.)

Few Greeks ever got to the point of denying the existence of
the supernatural completely. Indeed the great philosophers—
Socrates, Plato, and Aristotle—tried to deepen religious understanding and make it commensurate with their growing
intellectual sophistication. However, Plato's god—an infinite
being called the One—was not identifiable with any traditional
Greek deity, and Aristotle's Prime Mover was even less so.
However satisfying these concepts may have been philo-
sophically, their acceptance did away with Greek religion on the
practical level. Plato and Aristotle were secularists in that they
did not recognize a distinctively religious dimension to existence. Whatever religious obligations there might be were
discharged simply by living in accord with philosophical truths,
that is, by living in an enlightened, secular way.

Greek humanism, a trust in human capability and a celebration of human achievement, was a unique and powerful
contribution to Western civilization. Few, if any, other cultures

of the world developed quite the same perspective. To this day, for example, some of the great Eastern civilizations, notably India's, officially espouse a view of reality in which human existence counts for very little in the great expanse of eternity and man's life is ruled by inexorable forces over which he has no control.

Until nearly the time of Christ, the culture of the Hebrews and the culture of the Greeks had almost no contact with one other. It would have been reasonable to assume that they were basically incompatible, two widely divergent and ultimately contradictory approaches to life. They were, however, integrated by an entirely new movement—Christianity.

At first, the early Christians were wholly children of the Hebrew tradition. There was even debate in the early church over whether gentile converts had to be circumcised and observe the Jewish dietary laws. Before long, however, it became apparent not only that Christianity had to evangelize the gentiles ("Go forth and make disciples of all nations" [Mt 28:19]), but that non-Jews would be a more fertile ground for conversion than the Hebrews themselves.

The earliest Christian attempts to reach out to the Greek world (Greek was the common language of the Roman Empire) were probably motivated by the desire to make the gospel intelligible to the gentile mind. Thus already in John's Gospel the Son of God is called "the Word," the Greek philosophical concept "Logos." Before the end of the second century, Christianity had begun to produce teachers, like Justin the Martyr, who were at home in Greek philosophy.

However, one of the greatest of the early theologians, Tertullian, asked the famous rhetorical question, "What has Athens to do with Jerusalem?" The implied answer was "Nothing." Tertullian urged the position, revived periodically, that since Christian revelation contains all truth necessary to salvation, there is no need to dabble in pagan wisdom.

But Tertullian eventually left the church to join a rather obscure heretical sect. In time his position became a minority one. There have been, in every age, a majority of simple, believing Christians who have looked to divine revelation for authoritative guidance and have felt no need to pursue philosophical inquiries. The tradition of the scholarly believer, the man of faith who is also steeped in secular learning, became established quite early, though, and has persisted in most denominations until the present day. The greatest intellect of the period around 400 A.D. was Augustine of Hippo. He was equally learned in Christian doctrine and the writings of the pagan sages and was able to use the latter to deepen understanding of the former.

More was involved than rational inquiry alone, however. As it became clear that the second coming of Christ was not imminent and as Christians ceased to be persecuted but were given official recognition by the Roman Empire, they had to consider how to live in the world. Gradually they decided to take upon themselves worldly responsibilities as civil magistrates, merchants, lords of the land, craftsmen, teachers, etc. While never losing sight of their heavenly goal, they were not to neglect the earth. They were to strive to realize the teachings of Christ as far as possible in their daily lives. Hence the paradox of monasteries, supposedly peopled by men who had fled the world, being the centers of civilization during the Dark Ages. These were the places where secular as well as religious learning was taught and techniques of improved agriculture were developed.

Although the term was not often used, this amounted to a Christian humanism, the best of the Greek world (filtered through the Romans) placed in the service of religious faith. Augustine held that men were simultaneously citizens of two cities, that of God and that of man.

In the later centuries, Rome had become more overtly secular, more skeptical, and sometimes more mocking of religion than the Greeks had been. Although probably a majority of the inhabitants of the Empire continued to believe in the supernatural (new cults from the East were popular even in Rome), the first through the fifth centuries A.D. were a time of considerable cynicism, confusion, anxiety, and agnosticism.

Christianity was responsible for a major spiritual rebirth, and virtually the entire Western world became monotheistic, mostly Christian, with a small minority of Jews and eventually Moslems. For over a thousand years after A.D. 500 there was almost no atheism or serious religious skepticism in the West.

This is not to say that all problems ceased. It proved easier in theory than in practice to state the proper relationship between the things of God and the things of the world in politics, in economics, in family matters, etc. There are no finally definitive answers in any of those areas. Christians in each period of history have had to wrestle with living in the world without being of it.

The Catholic Church, which was virtually synonomous with Western Christianity until after 1500, had little trouble adapting all kinds of pagan creations to the uses of the faith—buildings, literary forms, legal and political structures, even much of the calendar (the celebration of the birth of Christ coincides with the traditional celebration of the Winter solstice, for example). But, intellectually there were serious problems. After 1100, the philosophy of Aristotle was gradually rediscovered, after having been lost to Europe during the Dark Ages. Aristotle seemed to present a fully developed, self-contained, invulnerable system which rationally explained the whole universe. There seemed to be no need for faith.

In the twelfth century, the enigmatic monk-philosopher Peter Abelard seemed to make logic into an absolute, so that whatever could not be proved or explained logically was deemed false. A few at least nominally Christian philosophers were willing to swallow Aristotle whole, either implicitly denying faith or sealing it in a watertight compartment.

However, the theologian Thomas Aquinas attempted a synthesis of Aristotle and Christian revelation. This synthesis was widely accepted in his own day and influential even to the present. Whatever might be thought of particular aspects of it, the attempt itself can be regarded as perhaps the most comprehensive effort ever made to forge a Christian humanism. Aquinas taught that, since God created the universe, what the universe reveals to human inquiry must be in harmony with divine revelation. Furthermore, since the human mind is made in the image of God, it is a reliable guide to truth. The ultimate truths of God are above human understanding, but there can be no real conflict between reason and revelation. A Christian can simultaneously be a man of faith and develop his human powers to the fullest. Ultimately the two will harmonize with and complement one another.

Aquinas' synthesis did not satisfy everyone. It began to come apart in the fourteenth century, mainly under the criticisms of philosophers like William of Ockham, who thought Aquinas had conceded too much to reason. In their view the human intellect is at best a rather feeble lantern. Most of them regarded the truths of faith as far more reliable than anything man can discover on his own.

Ostensibly, therefore, these philosophers (generally grouped under the category of Nominalists) were protecting faith. Unwittingly they revealed a dilemma which has always confronted Christian humanists. If the believer denigrates human achievement and human wisdom, he runs the risk of making faith seem irrelevant to life. Human powers are then allowed to develop independently of religion and will finally be in opposition to it. But, if the possibilities of human nature are accepted too easily, the radical nature of faith is in danger of being overlooked and the believer can slip into an easy worldliness. In a sense, and largely unintentionally, the Nominalists issued a declaration of the independence of philosophy from faith. Although the full implications of this would take several centuries to become apparent, they prepared the way for a purely secular intellectual life.

If Nominalism represented a denial of Christian humanism, in the same centuries (roughly 1350-1550) a new kind of humanism was emerging, intimately connected with the phase of Western cultural history called the Renaissance. Renaissance Humanism has often been misunderstood. Countless textbooks describe it as marking a turning away from the God-centered universe of the Middle Ages toward a man-centered universe.

Supposedly, people in the previous thousand years had lived for eternity but now began living for this world. Thus, so the popular argument runs, the Renaissance marked the beginning of modern secularism.

The historical reality was a great deal more complex. For one thing, there were practically no atheists in the Renaissance and hardly any people who were even skeptical of religion. The great majority of known Renaissance Humanists were believing Christians, mainly Catholics. Some of them were extremely devout. For example, Giovanni Pico della Mirandola, in some ways a very worldly individual and author of a famous manifesto of Humanism, *Oration on the Dignity of Man,* seriously considered becoming a monk just prior to his untimely death. Authors like Francesco Petrarch made strenuous efforts to synthesize their Christianity and their Humanism. Even Giovanni Boccaccio, who wrote the racy and quite profane *Decameron,* retracted those of his writings which had been a source of scandal.

Already during the Renaissance confusion over the meaning of the word "humanist" had set in. The only wholly satisfactory way of defining a Renaissance Humanist is in the narrowest sense of the word. He was somebody with a professional interest in the humanities—poetry, oratory, history, painting, sculpture, architecture, music—as distinct from philosophy, which Humanists regarded as too abstract and scientific to do justice to the complexities of human existence. They did not exclude theology from their interests. Instead they sought to develop a theology independent of Aristotelian philosophy.

But there were barely submerged snags in the Humanist program. Their love of literature and the arts carried them back to the Greeks and the Romans, whose achievements in those areas seemed more impressive and profound than anything that had been produced since. There was a strange contradiction here. The Humanists were professed and believing Christians who were forced into the position of saying that civilization, from a human standpoint, had started going downhill at the time of the triumph of Christianity.

They admired the architecture of Greek temples extrava-
gantly, and applied the term "Gothic" to medieval Christian
cathedrals to express their belief that such structures were
primitive and barbaric. Some Humanists confessed that they
found the Greek of the New Testament inferior to that of
Homer, the Latin of Augustine less delightful than that of
Cicero. Nor was it style alone that drew them back to the pagan
past. They also found in Cicero a noble, balanced, ripely wise
view of ethics. Some of them found it easier to identify with the
teachings of the Stoic emperor Marcus Aurelius than with the
monk Thomas à Kempis, whose *Imitation of Christ* eschewed
classical values both in style and content. For perhaps the
majority of Humanists, especially in Italy where the Renaissance reached its fullest flowering, a sincere, conscious,
explicit Christian faith was never successfully reconciled with
an admiration for the ancient pagans. In a sense, they were
Christians intellectually, pagans emotionally and imaginatively.

Today the Renaissance is celebrated more for its art than its
thought. There is no doubt that through its art an even more
frankly humanistic approach to life was expressed. From the
days of the Roman Empire until the fourteenth century, lifelike
portraits of people were almost unknown. Suddenly they
became common. The great artistic and architectural skills of
the Middle Ages had mostly gone into the construction and
decoration of churches. While religious art still flourished in the
Renaissance, the same skills were increasingly used in honoring
great families or important cities. Some of the most outstanding
Renaissance architecture was in palaces and town halls. For the
first time since antiquity the nude human body was once again
celebrated in all its perfection, as a kind of metaphor about
human nature itself.

The Italian city of Florence was the birthplace and chief
nursery of the Renaissance. The Florentines came to manifest
quite secular attitudes towards life. They approved money-
making as essential to leading the good life, took unabashed
delight in creature comforts, encouraged the development of

every kind of human talent for its own sake, and held up honor, fame, power, and prestige as worthy goals. The most extreme statement of this was Niccolo Machiavelli's amoral political treatise, *The Prince,* which shocked many people but was only an extension of attitudes already widespread in Renaissance Italy.

Yet the Florentines, as other Italians of the time, were also pious. Near the end of their Renaissance, the friar Girolamo Savanarola preached what amounted to a fire-and-brimstone revival in the city and persuaded sophisticated Florentines to throw their worldly "vanities," including valuable paintings and books, into a huge bonfire. The same apparent contradictions were found at the papal court in Rome. The highly sophisticated popes of the Renaissance were great patrons of the arts and of learning. Although they might have been expected to suppress pagan tendencies among the Humanists, by the late fifteenth century the popes themselves were being drawn in the same direction. Savanarola was burnt at the stake on orders of the notorious Pope Alexander VI. Alexander's openly immoral life reflected the easy worldliness in high church circles. This had developed to some extent from an attitude which worshipped beauty divorced from morality and was more under the imaginative sway of the ancient pagans than of Scripture. Yet Alexander too was a believer and even, in his way, somewhat devout.

It cannot, therefore, be argued that the Renaissance ushered in the modern age of secularism in the West. Certainly, that was far from the Humanists' intentions. They would have been shocked if it had been suggested that they were weakening religious faith. In a sense, the Renaissance raised premature questions which it could not itself answer. The most important of these was how believing and practicing Christians could allow full sway to their natural human impulses. Up until then, with an almost unanimous voice, Christianity had taught an ethic of self-control, self-denial, and deliberate efforts to transcend the merely human. The Humanists did not deny this ethic openly, but they lived as though it were not always true. They did not think much about the consequences of their way of life.

Young men from Northern Europe repaired to Italy with great frequency during the fifteenth and early sixteenth centuries. Some of these Northerners were shocked at the rather profane lives and opinions of the Italian Humanists. Some of them were also troubled by the Italians' apparent failure to reconcile their Christianity and their Humanism. They went home determined to remedy that failure.

The greatest of the Northern Humanists was Erasmus of Rotterdam. He was a humanist in the strict sense of the word, a scholar of languages and literature. He also shared the Italian Humanists' distaste for abstract philosophy, and hence found himself alienated from the prevailing theology of the Catholic Church, which made use of Aristotle as filtered through Aquinas.

Erasmus was practically the inventor of what came to be called Christian Humanism, which at a minimum meant the application of scholarly tools to the study not of pagan but of Christian texts, especially the Bible. Erasmus' aim was to kindle a stronger piety by leading Christians to a deeper and more authentic understanding of their faith.

Paradoxically, this Christian Humanism probably led to the weakening of a specifically Catholic faith, since Erasmus' emphasis on the study of the Bible tended to produce a personal, somewhat individualistic faith that was not always in harmony with church teaching. Overall, Erasmus found in the Scripture a simple, basically ethical kind of Christianity. While he did not deny the major teachings and practices of the Catholic Church, he called many of them into question and seemed to suggest that the great and elaborate structure of the church was really unnecessary. Later he ruefully noted that people were saying that "Erasmus laid the egg that Luther hatched."

Yet Erasmus remained a Catholic, albeit a rather marginal one, until his death. He opposed the Protestant Reformation on

Desiderius Erasmus (1466-1536), often known as Erasmus of Rotterdam, is one of the best examples of a Christian Humanist. In the period of the Renaissance (roughly 1350-1550), the term "humanist" was not used primarily to indicate someone who exalted the importance of man at the expense of God but someone who was interested in humanistic studies—literature, art, politics—which pertained to the total behavior of human beings. Although Erasmus' religious beliefs were sometimes ambiguous, he was a believing Christian and did a great deal to encourage the study of the Bible.

several grounds, especially because it shattered the unity of the church. The other great Northern Humanist, Erasmus' good friend Thomas More, became a vigorous apologist for Catholic orthodoxy and died rather than deny the Pope's authority in England. More has always had great appeal, in part because he seemed to exemplify humanist attitudes. He was a married layman, active in politics, a social critic, a great wit, an accomplished stylist, a man who seems to have enjoyed life. Yet he had seriously thought of becoming a monk, became completely disillusioned with politics, and had a strong and lively sense of the transiency of all worldly things and the need to live for eternity.

The Renaissance, at least in the South, had largely passed its peak by the time of the Protestant Reformation. In any case, it can be said with accuracy that the Reformation effectively pushed the Renaissance off the stage of history, and postponed indefinitely the consideration of the questions which the Renaissance had raised.

Martin Luther had little acquaintance with Renaissance Humanism and even less sympathy for it. Ulrich Zwingli, Philip Melanchthon, and John Calvin had been Humanists, but Humanism did not appreciably influence their development of theology or piety. In a sense it could be argued that the Reformation was anti-humanistic, in that the doctrines of the sinfulness of man and salvation through faith alone effectively prevented any reliance on human powers. Erasmus had an acrimonious debate with Luther over human free will, Erasmus defending and Luther vigorously denying it. The more radical Reformers were also anti-humanistic in that they excluded the arts from worship almost entirely, although Luther made a major exception for music. Whereas Catholic theology had generally developed some kind of synthesis with pagan philosophy, the Reformers eschewed all such connections in favor of the "pure" Word of God.

In another sense, however, Protestantism can be said to have encouraged Humanism by its denial of monasticism. Henceforth, the only Christian vocation would be the vocation to live in the world. Marriage and family came to be both normative and ideal. Worldly occupations took on a new, religious significance. It has even been argued that, by a rather complex route, Calvinism justified modern capitalism and the pursuit of wealth. If the typical Catholic figure of the Middle Ages had been the robed monk in his cell, the typical Protestant figure of early modern times was the black-suited businessman in a Rembrandt painting, sitting on the board of some civic organization.

In the sixteenth century almost all passion—intellectual, moral, personal, even political—was drawn into religious conflict. Whether one was Catholic or Protestant mattered crucially, because eternal salvation and fidelity to Christ were at stake. Even as they contended sometimes violently, Catholics and Protestants still agreed on the fundamentals of faith—the Trinity, the divinity of Christ, the authority of Scripture (however interpreted), miracles, the Ten Commandments, etc. Whatever cautious secular voices had been raised during the Renaissance were all but drowned out during the Reformation. Unbelief seemed almost unthinkable. What mattered was the kind of belief one espoused. An observer of the Western scene in 1550 might reasonably have concluded that all trends towards secularization had been permanently ended. The West was so deeply and passionately religious that its entire future would be shaped by the competing faiths.

Yet this religious passion which burned so brightly could be viewed like the flaring up of a fire just before it starts to go out. The roots of secularization in the West had been spreading for some time, and certain developments of the Reformation period were, unrecognized at the time, helping them to push shoots above the ground.

THREE

The Secularization of the West

THE GREAT RELIGIOUS upheaval of the sixteenth century contributed to the long-term decline of religion and the rise of secularism in the West, although few of the participants could have foreseen this at the time.

Perhaps the most important effect was the reality of religious division itself. Beginning in the late sixteenth century, Western Christians had to begin to cope with the reality of what would later be called pluralism. Now such pluralism is usually discussed with respect to religious values in public life, but there is a deeper problem which it poses and which is often overlooked. In the midst of a continually multiplying number of groups claiming to have the truth, it becomes difficult for many people to believe that any faith can be true. During the religious wars in France, for example, the essayist Michel de Montaigne, though at least a nominal Catholic, expressed a certain skepticism about all religion. He wondered how the people on opposite sides of the wars could be so certain of their beliefs. The fact that people held to contradictory beliefs with dogmatic certitude was, for Montaigne, grounds for wondering how either side could be right.

His attitude was not widely shared by his contemporaries, but in the next century it came to be expressed more openly. Put simply, the argument of the incipient skeptics was, "If a variety of religious groups each claims to have the truth, and each claims that all the others are in error, does it not seem reasonable that *all* of them are in error?"

The wars and persecutions which accompanied the religious divisions also had an important effect on the growth of skepticism. The spectacle of bloody violence and hatred directed by Christians at other Christians decade after decade took its toll. The religious wars in Europe lasted from roughly 1540 to 1700. Although they always had political causes as well, religion usually provided the passion and the chief justification for the fighting. Religious persecution was practiced in virtually every Western country until after 1700. One does not often judge the teachings of a religion by the conduct of the people who do not live up to them. However, in the seventeenth and eighteenth centuries, religion did appear as a destructive force, and this certainly had a deep psychological effect.

The reaction was not usually outright skepticism, although there was some of that. More common was a half-conscious decision by many Christians to dampen the passions which their faith generated. Insofar as those passions were murderous, this was a genuinely Christian thing to do. However, religious belief, since it is supposed to infuse the believer's whole life, must transform his being in profound ways. Some religious and political leaders of the late seventeenth century decided, more or less deliberately, to encourage a bland, formal, nearly contentless religion which could never arouse sufficient emotions to threaten disorder.

From the period just before 1700 we can date a familiar type of modern Christianity. It stresses ethical teachings, denigrates the importance of basic doctrines, relegates belief to people's private lives, and is embarrassed by open displays of religious fervor. The familiar modern social convention appeared whereby it is considered bad manners to discuss religion, in part because it is likely to be divisive. Religious toleration came to mean not only allowing others to practice their faith but never implying that their faith might be incomplete or that some matters of truth cannot be ignored.

England was probably the place where such attitudes were most clearly manifest after about 1690. England had two revolutions in the seventeenth century, one of them accompanied by a civil war. Especially in the first one (1642-1660), religion played a major role. An ardent Puritanism was pitted against the Anglican monarchy. Beginning in the late seventeenth century, many Englishmen espoused a religious philosophy called Latitudinarianism which, as the name implies, was a style of church life broad enough to encompass almost everyone. For the next 150 years, membership in the Anglican Church was a social necessity involving minimum conformity to its public observances. But any kind of open religious fervor, anything that smacked of what was called "enthusiasm," was held in disdain. It was in reaction to this aridity that the Methodist movement began.

By itself the fragmentation of Christianity and the bitter conflicts which accompanied it would probably not have produced the secularization of the West. There were other forces at work, the long-term effects of which were only dimly recognized at the time. The most important of these was probably the growth of science.

In 1543, the Polish astronomer Nicholas Copernicus published a book in which he challenged the ancient theory that the earth is the center of the universe. He claimed that the sun is the center and the earth merely a planet. It took sixty years for the new theory to become widely known even in educated circles, but by the early seventeenth century it was the subject of much controversy. The Italian scientist Galileo Galilei was condemned by the Catholic Church for teaching the Copernican theory.

Protestants and Catholics both resisted the new theory because it seemed to contradict the Scripture, which speaks of the sun moving in the heavens. There were other problems as well. Not the least of these was that man had been dethroned from a central place in the universe and was now a mere inhabitant of one of the planets. The image of the cosmos which had been almost universally held for two millenia was called into question, and people wondered about other beliefs handed down from the past.

It would take man a long time to work out the problem of reconciling scriptural authority with scientific discovery. Many more conflicts (for example, over the age of the universe) would arise in the next three centuries. Though many of them had the effect of weakening the credibility of religious authority only slightly, their cumulative effect was powerful.

It would be a mistake, however, to regard the Scientific Revolution as leading directly to secularization. The leading scientists (Galileo and Isaac Newton, for example) were devout. Almost all scientists were at least conventional believers. Indeed, Newton thought that the laws of physics which he formulated made the existence of God more certain rather than less so, since only a Supreme Intelligence could have created such a marvellously ordered and rational universe.

The philosophers inspired by the new science, like Francis Bacon and René Descartes, took pains to protect religious belief from skeptical attack. Their very act of protecting it helped subtly to undermine it. They seemed to imply that faith could not withstand rational scrutiny and was primarily a matter of subjective choice. Descartes prided himself on developing a rigorous proof for the existence of God. But his fellow Frenchman Blaise Pascal, as great a mathematician as Descartes and a fervent Christian apologist, asked whether "the god of the geometers" had anything to do with the "God of Abraham, Isaac, and Jacob." (Pascal, precociously, also foresaw that science might become anti-humanistic, by reducing man to a mere speck in the vastness of the universe.)

From the beginning of the European universities in the twelfth century, theology had been the "queen of the sciences," and religion had been seen as at the center of reality. Now thinkers like Descartes "protected" religion by putting it off to one side. Descartes regarded mathematics as the most perfect of disciplines, the one which provided a hope of certitude in other areas of inquiry. Others looked to other sources, such as empirical investigation. Religion was not openly attacked nor, for the most part, was it disbelieved. It just ceased to be important. The dramatic success of the new science stimulated an enormous sense of self-confidence in many people. They assumed that the scientific method would in time unravel all mysteries, solve all problems. Religion was increasingly felt as something unnecessary even if true, to be shunted into a side room of one's life.

If the seventeenth century still treated Christianity with respect, the eighteenth century opened a frontal attack on it. The *philosophes* (probably best translated as "intellectuals") were self-proclaimed apostles of an "Enlightenment." This term implies the existence of prior darkness, largely the result of Christianity, which was equated with superstition and ignorance. In their mental world there was no room for mystery or the supernatural. Whatever could not be discovered or proven rationally was false.

In the eighteenth century, for the first time since Roman days, there were self-proclaimed atheists, though atheism was not fully respectable even in advanced intellectual circles. Most of the intellectuals were Deists, meaning that they believed in a God like Newton's Supreme Intelligence, who had planned and created the marvellously well-ordered universe. But, after creating it, this "clock-maker God" had left it to run in accordance with its own laws.

There was no divine providence or miracles—God did not "interfere" in his creation. Nor did he reveal himself to his people, in the Scriptures or through the church. All of man's knowledge of God came through his creation, by means of rational inquiry. There was thus no need for formal religion; in fact, formal religion was based on falsehood. One "worshipped" God only by living in accord with reason. Prayer was meaningless. The Bible, while it contained some elevated and inspiring passages, was considered a hodge-podge of man-made tales, many of them actually harmful if believed. For the most part the intellectuals of the eighteenth century held to a morality quite similar to Judaeo-Christian morality, but they derived it solely

François Arouet (1694-1778), who wrote under the name of Voltaire, was one of the first Western intellectuals to make a full-scale attack on traditional Judaism and Christianity. He believed in God, but in the so-called "deistic" sense, which meant a remote and abstract god who did not "meddle" in the affairs of the world he had created. In common with other "advanced" thinkers of his time, Voltaire thought organized religion was an evil social influence which ought to be curtailed in every way possible. Of the Old Testament he wrote, "This is what fools have written, what imbeciles comment, what rogues teach, and what young children are made to learn by heart. And the scholar who is filled with indignation and who is irritated by the most abominable absurdities that have ever disgraced human nature, is called blasphemer!"

from reason and recognized no religious authority in moral matters. Some of them believed in the possibility of an afterlife but many did not.

By the middle of the eighteenth century, the basic outlines of modern Secular Humanism had been expressed most wittily and influentially by the French writer Voltaire. There was one major difference from modern Secular Humanism: Voltaire could quip that "If God did not exist, he would have to be invented." Most intellectuals of the time thought it unreasonable not to believe in a God, although this was not, as Pascal had foreseen a century earlier, the God of Christian revelation.

The anti-religious sentiment of the Enlightenment was not solely a matter of ideas. Voltaire also often said about the Catholic Church, "Crush the infamous thing!" In all the Western societies, education was largely the responsibility of the churches, and the churches, established by law, were highly influential. Thus the anti-Christian intellectuals also opposed the church as an institution and a social force. The statement "I disagree with what you say, but I will defend to the death your right to say it," though often attributed to Voltaire, did not represent his views accurately. He was willing to use coercion against his intellectual enemies.

As far back as the Reformation a few people had, for religious reasons, advocated complete religious toleration. Later, many people espoused limited religious toleration as a way of avoiding destructive civil wars. In the eighteenth century, the intellectuals began to advocate religious toleration as a matter of principle. Their motives were somewhat mixed. In part they urged religious toleration out of respect for individual conscience. In part, however, it was out of the conviction that all religious beliefs were equally false and thus all should be equally tolerated. Voltaire rejoiced that, in a society where there were many religious groups, all of them would be weak.

Probably no more than about a tenth of Europe's population was seriously affected by Enlightenment ideas in the eighteenth century. (Indeed, Voltaire tried to keep those ideas from the masses. He thought they were not ready for them.) But, among the educated classes they were highly influential. By about 1770, it was fashionable to scoff at organized relgion and its teachings.

Although the intellectuals of the time portrayed the churches as reactionary enemies of progress, those churches offered surprisingly feeble resistance to the Enlightenment onslaught. In England, except for a few groups like the Methodists, religion slumbered and was content with mere formal adherence. Of this situation Voltaire heartily approved. At one point he raised a storm by claiming that the Clavinist clergy of Geneva secretly agreed with him. In Catholic France the higher clergy were particularly worldly. Many of them viewed the church mainly as a career, and not a few were eager to embrace Enlightenment ideas, no matter how destructive of Christianity. It was not the last time secularism triumphed by the passivity and even active cooperation of the supposed guardians of the faith.

The French Revolution of 1789 accomplished many of the goals of the englightenment, sweeping away by violence all the social institutions to which the intellectuals objected, including the church. Most of the leading *philosophes* were dead by then; the few still alive found that their ideas did not save them from prison and even execution. If they approved of many of the goals of the Revolution, they did not approve its methods. They had believed in reason, but the Revolution seemed to be the triumph of violent passions and hatreds.

If the Revolution was in one sense the fulfillment of the Enlightenment, it was in another sense its repudiation. It destroyed the *philosophes'* dream that, having given up religious authority, man could remake his life peacefully and tolerantly. Instead, discrediting all traditional authorities ushered in a period of near anarchy. During the so-called Reign of Terror, thousands of Frenchmen were summarily guillotined. Most of them were probably innocent of any crime, and few of them had been given even the semblance of a fair trial. The Terror, an orgy of hate and revenge, was strong disproof of the Enlightenment belief that man, left to himself, would inevitably behave in a rational and just way. The dark side of human nature asserted itself with a literal vengeance in the mid-1790s.

The Terror was the first example of a familiar modern phenomenonon: a movement to remake the world in the name of humanity gives birth to a murderous and destructive fanaticism. Every modern revolution has borne the same witness. It is one of the strongest arguments against total reliance on man and his goodwill. It has also given rise, among thoughtful people, to a strong distrust of all movements which proclaim that they have the welfare of "humanity" at heart. Time and again, this has meant the crushing of individual human beings in the name of a political abstraction.

The facts of the revolutionary Terror are well-known, yet their implications have not been widely recognized. Secular Humanists have often manipulated public opinion in their favor by charging that religion has a history of bloody persecution, while Humanism has always been tolerant. When they want to invoke the specter of murderous intolerance they talk about either the Catholic Inquisition or the "witch-burnings" carried out by both Catholics and Protestants. Rarely is there reference to the "Committees of Public Safety," which implemented the Reign of Terror in the name of humanity.

Modern Secular Humanism has been stained with blood from its very birth. At first, the Revolution seemed willing to tolerate the church if the clergy would promise to be loyal to the regime. Soon the government embarked on a systematic "de-Christianizing" campaign. Churches were closed and converted to profane uses, like stables for horses. Religious symbols were destroyed. The religious press was outlawed. All religious services were forbidden. Priests and nuns were rounded up in large numbers and sent into exile, imprisoned, or executed. The aim of the government was to wipe out every remaining vestige of Christianity.

Although its full fury was found in France, similar ideas and practices spread to other parts of Europe where the Revolution itself spread. It became, in time, a permanent feature of European life. Since the Revolution, there have been few

Charles Darwin (1809-92) had an immense impact on Western civilization through his theories of evolution and natural selection. At first many religious believers opposed Darwin's theories, although later they came to be widely accepted. Darwin himself at one time studied to be a minister. However, as he grew older his faith all but disappeared, and he eventually wrote, "I can indeed hardly see how anyone ought to wish Christianity to be true."

instances of physical persecution directed against believers in the West. However, in France and Spain in particular, certain political parties, when in power, have closed religious schools and done all they could to harass the church and destroy its influence. For the most part, the people responsible for such policies could subscribe to the tenets of the two *Humanist Manifestoes*.

The restoration of the European monarchies in 1815 was generally accompanied by a religious revival. In part this was in reaction to the suppression of religion during the Revolution. In part, however, it was also out of the belief that the philosophy of the Enlightenment had itself been narrow and restrictive. It had not taken account of the depth and complexity of human nature. The dominant cultural movement of the early nineteenth century was Romanticism which, in general, emphasized the profound mysteries of existence. While many Romantics were no more friendly to the church than the Enlightenment had been, some became ardent believers.

Christianity in the Western world may have reached its low point in the eighteenth century. The nineteenth century produced a situation rather like two elevators passing each other, one going up, the other down. There was a widespread religious revival, both in Protestant and in Catholic countries, all through the nineteenth century. The Oxford Movement in England, whose leading figure was John Henry Newman, is one of the best known. Religious belief and churchgoing were once again respectable, and in some circles mandatory. There were important Christian intellectuals, like Newman and the Danish Lutheran Søren Kierkegaard, which the eighteenth century had lacked.

But the implications of eighteenth-century secularism continued to be developed, in more and more radical ways. The French Revolution established what amounted to a permanent party dedicated to using political power, when it could, for the systematic expunging of religious influence from public life. Science too continued moving in directions sometimes damaging to religion, though some leading scientists (like Louis

Pasteur and Gregor Mendel) were devout believers. Besides the conflict over the authority of the Bible (centered now on the creation account in the book of Genesis), there developed in the nineteenth century what has been called "scientism." This holds that only science has the key to truth and that whatever is not scientific is false. Nineteenth-century science sometimes held up the promise of solving all human problems, rendering religion obsolete in the process.

Only gradually were the practical benefits of science, in the form of useful technology, discovered. In the nineteenth century industrial technology came into its own, and it developed its own cult. The avante garde held that in time the practical application of science, through the invention of the right kinds of machines, would solve all human problems. Technology gave to some people such an immense sense of self-confidence that dependence on God came to seem meaningless.

The nineteenth century also gave birth to three new revolutionary systems of thought, those identified with Karl Marx, Charles Darwin, and Sigmund Freud. What all three shared, different though they were in many respects, was a basic materialism. Human existence was described, respectively, by economic necessities, biological evolution, and sexual urges.

All three movements gave further impetus to Secular Humanism in that all three dispensed with God. Marx was a militant atheist. Darwin did not reject God out of necessity, but as he grew older he became more and more a skeptic. Freud regarded religious belief as a neurotic illusion. Yet, in a sense, all three can also be called anti-humanistic, helping to reveal some of the internal contradictions of Humanism itself. Since the days of the Greeks, men had prided themselves on their spiritual and rational natures. This was at the basis of authentic Humanism. Marx seemed to say that most rational thought was a mere cover for economic self-interest. Knowingly or unknowingly, men acted in accord with class interests over which they had no control. Darwin and his followers were never able to resolve man's exact relationship to the animal kingdom or determine

Sigmund Freud (1856-1939) had immense influence in theorizing about the disorders of the human mind and methods of coping with them. Positing certain sexual drives as at the heart of human behavior, he gave new direction to anti-religious opinion by holding that all religion was itself the result of neurosis. After him, perhaps a majority of psychotherapists have either ignored religion or dealt with it as a disorder. Freud wrote of religious dogmas that "they are illusions, fulfillments of the oldest, strongest, and most insistent wishes of mankind."

how much dignity he could claim by virtue of transcending his animal nature. Freud treated almost all conscious thought as misleading and saw human nature as shaped by unconscious drives of which man had little accurate understanding and even less control.

The few passing moves towards atheism that had occurred prior to 1800 had been turned aside. The Enlightenment itself had erected a bulwark against it. In the nineteenth century, atheism came into its own. The focus had also shifted, subtly but importantly. Earlier atheists were mostly people who thought that there was no rational basis for believing in God. Nineteenth-century atheists argued that belief in God was undesirable. In effect, they willed not to believe in him.

Marx proclaimed atheism as a necessity. All religious belief reflected unjust social structures. Belief in God would necessarily distract people from the struggle for social revolution. The philosopher Ludwig Feuerbach, roughly Marx's contemporary and a major influence on him, argued that mankind would remain forever in a kind of childlike state so long as belief in God persisted. It was left for the philosopher Friederich Nietzsche, later in the century, to proclaim the "death of God," by which he meant the death of the idea of God. Nietzsche postulated the Superman who, without the benefit of divine authority or objective moral law, would make his own values and decree the kind of world he would live in.

The strain of modern Humanism which comes down through Feuerbach, Marx, and Nietzsche can be called Promethean Humanism, after the figure in Greek mythology who stole fire from the gods to give it to man. It is a Humanism which bases itself on rebellion and a denial of God. It would counter Voltaire, "If God exists, he must be destroyed." The older, somewhat gentler Humanism deriving from the Enlightenment is less passionate. It was content to say that there is no rational evidence for believing in God.

Enlightenment Humanism had always prided itself on its morality. Its proudest boast has been that, without the sanction of religion, its moral code has been very similar to that of

Friedrich Nietzsche (1844-1900) fashioned a philosophy of rebellion—against God and against all accepted morality—in the name of an emergent "superman" who would be free of all restraints on his behavior and would create his own truth. Nietzsche wrote, "Christianity should not be beautiful or embellished; it has waged deadly war against this higher type of man. . . . Christianity has sided with all that is weak and base, with all failures."

Christianity. But the new Humanism of the nineteenth century embodied a demonic urge to negate and destroy. As Nietzsche saw clearly, it was not only a matter of not believing in God. Once God had been denied, man could achieve true freedom only by denying all moral constraints on himself and inventing his own morality. The human will alone became sovereign. This type of Humanism has often descended into Nihilism, the urge to destroy and annihilate every accepted good. The older, more genteel kind of Humanism has been steadily losing ground to this newer kind, which is in essence profoundly anti-humanistic.

The major intellectual bases for Secular Humanism had mostly been laid by the middle of the nineteenth century. Besides new and revolutionary ideas, the nineteenth century marked the beginning of the age of mass communications. For the first time in history, a majority of the population, at least in some countries, could read and write. Mass-circulation newspapers, magazines, and books began to be published. Most Western nations made at least a beginning toward establishing compulsory education for all children. In addition, most remaining censorship was either abolished or severely curtailed.

The result was that ideas which in the eighteenth century had been confined to an educated elite now started to gain common currency. For a long time they were resisted. Popular culture in the West remained conservative with respect to religious and moral values. But gradually the movement spread. Organizations of self-proclaimed atheists or humanists were established. In the 1880s, an atheist was elected to the English Parliament. After attempts to deny him his seat because he could not swear the customary oath, he was allowed to serve.

America has shared in the general secularization of the West, but it has followed its own path in certain ways. It deserves special consideration.

FOUR

The American Experience

O F THE MANY NATIONS founded in modern times, few have had as strongly religious a heritage as the United States of America. As every schoolchild knows, many of the early settlers of the continent were fervent Christians seeking freedom to worship according to conscience—not only the Puritans of New England, but also the Quakers of Pennsylvania, the Catholics of Maryland, and a number of other groups. Since the earliest settlements of North America were also made during a very intensely religious period in Western history, virtually all the settlers were believing and practicing Christians. Most of the Atlantic seaboard was settled by English Protestants. French Catholics settled the Mississippi Valley and Spanish Catholics Florida, the Southwest, and California. By the time of the American Revolution, virtually all the colonies on the continent had at least a quasi-official church.

But the American Revolution occurred at the climax of the Enlightenment, and Enlightenment ideas greatly influenced the founding of the new nation.

The nation was originally the largely Protestant colonies of the Eastern seaboard; only later were predominantly Catholic areas admitted to the Union. But by 1775, much of the Protestant elite of those Eastern colonies had ceased to be orthodox Christians in the way their ancestors had been. This was especially true of the gentlemen planters of Virginia, who played a major role in the establishment of the new nation. Some, notably Thomas Jefferson, seem to have been Deists.

They believed in a Supreme Being and a moral law based on reason, but not in divine revelation. Others, like George Washington, were nominal Anglicans according to the familiar English pattern of the time. They maintained at least a loose affiliation with the church but did not seem to make religion an important part of their lives. In the North, the stern Puritanism of the seventeenth century had been modified to the point where many leading New Englanders could be called Deists.

There were thus certain paradoxes in the spirit of the new nation. The Declaration of Independence forthrightly acknowledged dependence on God; the Constitution did not mention him. America was in some ways a very religious nation, but, especially among its leaders, this religion was often ambiguous.

Most of the Founding Fathers, to one degree or another, were fearful of the possibility of religious conflict, intolerance, and persecution. There had been instances of these in colonial America. The examples from Europe were more numerous and more disturbing. These founders hit upon a radical new experiment—a nation whose basic structure guaranteed freedom of worship for all inhabitants and forbade any union of church and state. (The First Amendment to the Constitution reads in part: "Congress shall make no law respecting an establishment of religion, nor prohibiting the free exercise thereof.") This was a great benefit for the people of the new nation. Virtually nowhere in the world at the time was complete freedom of worship permitted and nowhere were citizens free from the obligation to support a church whose teachings they might find unacceptable.

There were certain ambiguities. Not only did the Founding Fathers desire to protect freedom and to allow all faiths to flourish; some of them were also motivated by a suspicion of all religion. This was especially true of Jefferson, who placed his stamp on so much early American thought. In many ways Jefferson's outlook was not appreciably different from Voltaire's, except that he was less outspoken in his antireligious sentiments. He wanted to confine religion to narrow

Thomas Jefferson (1743-1826) was one of the most important of America's Founding Fathers, and his opinions did much to shape the future direction of the nation. A nominal Anglican, Jefferson, in the manner of Voltaire, deeply distrusted almost all forms of organized religion and can be seen as the founder of a school of opinion which, in the name of neutrality, seeks to impose a kind of irreligion as the public norm. Typical of Jefferson's privately expressed opinions was his reference to the Trinity as "the hocus pocus phantasm of a God like another Cerberus, with one body and three heads." He added: "I confidently expect that the present generation will see Unitarianism become the general religion of the United States."

spheres of largely private life, out of a fear that public manifestations of religion would lead to strife and possible bloodshed. Some of the Founding Fathers, again Jefferson for one, simply believed the teachings of traditional Christianity to be false except where they coincided with Enlightenment ideas. They tolerated the various "sects," as they called them, but did not respect these groups nor regard their existence as particularly beneficial to the nation.

Thus from the beginning of the United States there has been a fundamental ambiguity with regard to official attitudes toward religion, ambiguities which only began to cause serious problems after World War II.

If the elite group of Founding Fathers had been representative of public opinion in 1789, America would have developed as a secular nation. There was, however, a fairly wide gap between them and the masses of the people; Enlightenment ideas usually spread only among a small minority. As nearly as can be determined, formal church membership was fairly low at the time, perhaps proportionately lower than it is now. But most historians think Americans of the time were religious even if unchurched. Earlier in the century there had begun in New England the Great Awakening. Great numbers of people responded to fervent preaching, repented of their sins, and resolved to live a new life. Early in the next century, there took place a Second Great Awakening, this one embracing the frontier as well. Smaller local manifestations of the same piety were common.

By about 1820, the spirit of the Enlightenment had waned in America, as it had in Europe. Later generations of leaders were more likely to be professing Christians than Deists. The Enlightenment influence did remain in certain respects and had significant long-term effects, but the public spirit of the nation was definitely religious.

Foreign visitors, like the perceptive Frenchman, Alexis de Tocqueville, remarked on the frequency with which God, divine providence, the Bible, and other religious themes were invoked in public. This sometimes gave rise to suspicions that politicians, for example, were using religion for their own ends. But whatever the abuses, religion was taken very seriously in America. Many Americans believed their nation the recipient of a special divine mandate.

Clearly, America had always been a nation of immigrants. At the time of its founding in 1789, the Atlantic seaboard was mainly Protestant and of British extraction. Culturally it looked to England. From the 1830s until at least the First World War, however, America was transformed almost beyond recognition by countless waves of immigrants from Europe. Some of these were "Free Thinkers," a nineteenth-century term roughly equivalent to "Secular Humanist." Most, however, were at least nominally religious, and many were a great deal more than nominal. Although economic privation was probably the chief motive for immigration, many had experienced either discrimination or persecution on account of their faith and were looking for an atmosphere of freedom. They treasured their religious beliefs and practices, and, if anything, the experience of the New World made them more devout.

By the time of the Civil War, religious influence in American life was pervasive. This went well beyond Fourth of July rhetoric (important though that rhetoric was for symbolic purposes). For one thing, religion provided the motive and the justification for most public expressions of morality. The anti-slavery movement, to take the chief example, had very religious roots. On the other side, the slave-owners justified their practice by appeals to the Bible and divine law. Although cynics might say that Christianity encouraged such irreconcilable divisions, the controversy over slavery showed the great seriousness with which religion was taken. Seemingly few Americans could tolerate living in a way they thought contrary to divine law. They at least had to rationalize their conduct.

After the Civil War, American society was transformed in profound and lasting ways by the completion of the Industrial Revolution begun several decades earlier. Although it was not until about 1920 that a majority of Americans could be classified as city-dwellers, the shift to the cities was already marked by the

1870s. Along with urbanization came everything that it implied, including a factory system which provided the principal employment. The successive waves of immigrants were absorbed into an expanding industrial system.

The American experience of the century after the Civil War belies the most widely accepted sociological explanation of secularization as a result of technological change and industrialization. According to this theory, religion is associated with older, more stable, predominantly agricultural ways of life. It is part of the inheritance of that way of life and not much questioned. It is further argued that the farmer, utterly dependent on the vagaries of nature, has a strong sense of his necessary reliance on God. Urbanization and industrialization disrupted this age-old pattern of living. Uprooted people belong to no clear community and experience no social pressure to conform. Finally, technology leads man to believe that the solutions to all problems lie within his grasp; all he needs is to work harder and become yet more ingenious.

This theory of secularization does seem to apply to large areas of the Old World. To a great extent the working classes of Western Europe fell away from religion in the nineteenth and twentieth centuries. However, this likely had less to do with industrialization than with the rigidity of traditional social organization; workers tended to identify religion with a state church and the aristocracy. Social and economic discontent thus tended to lead to a rejection of religion.

In the United States, ultimately the greatest industrial nation in the world, this did not happen. By and large, the working classes in America remained at least as religious as any other group, and more than some. A high proportion of immigrants prior to World War I were Catholics, and the Catholic Church was remarkably successful in ministering to them. In some ways, Catholics in America were more devout than they had been in Europe. A concrete proof of this devotion was the ability of a generally poor community to found and maintain a huge school system, from kindergartens to universities. On the Protestant side, the phenomenon of the revival was especially important. Evangelism of all kinds, some of it through the churches, was a major feature of popular culture in America. Possibly millions of people were led to religion, or strengthened in it, by this means. It was a phenomenon for which there was scant parallel anywhere else in the world.

America also proved itself religious in that it was fertile ground for new faiths. The number of new churches founded in the United States since the early nineteenth century is literally uncountable. By 1970, several thousand distinct Christian denominations could be identified, most of them quite small. But America has also produced some major and enduring religious movements like Mormonism, Jehovah's Witnesses, Christian Science, and the entire pentecostalist movement.

From before the Civil War until World War II, the broad religious outline of American life could be sketched fairly easily. America was a society in which a majority of people were at least formally affiliated with a church and many were active. Christian morality was almost universally accepted in principle and was taken as the appropriate guide to conduct. Even most non-church members believed in God and were respectful of the Bible and other kinds of religious authority. Church membership tended to ebb and flow, and religious leaders worried from time to time about the secularization of society, but at almost any time down to 1945 religion appeared to be in a healthy state.

Sociological theory would suggest that after the war there would be a decline in religious belief and practice, as often happens. Again America proved an exception. Perhaps partly because the war was viewed almost universally as morally justified and partly because of the material privations Americans had been suffering since 1929 (first the Great Depression, then the War itself), the country in 1945 seemed determined to build a stable society on solid values. The post-war world, down to about 1965, was very family-oriented. There was much concern with proper moral values, not only with respect to private morality, but also to long-standing social evils like segregation. The Civil Rights Movement was strongly religious in inspiration and leadership. Appeals to religious principles proved by far the most effective way of persuading people to reexamine their prejudices.

Adlai Stevenson, twice an unsuccessful candidate for the Presidency in the 1950s, once quipped, "I find Paul appealing and Peale appalling." The reference was to the popular preacher Norman Vincent Peale, who had endorsed Stevenson's opponent. Stevenson's comment may have been unfair, but it did indicate a problem with the official piety of the post-war era. In retrospect, it carried the seeds of its own destruction. Norman Vincent Peale achieved fame with books like *The Power of Positive Thinking*. Essentially he preached a faith which was happy, optimistic, and forward-looking. There was not much emphasis on sin or the need for repentance and almost no indication of the inner religious struggle that has characterized virtually every great figure in the history of Christianity. Peale, echoed by preachers all over America, in essence told people how to use religion to be happy.

Orthodox Christianity was by no means dead in the 1950s. But often unrecognized, subtle distortions of the Christian message were creeping even into churches which had been traditionally rather conservative. Religion was represented as a good thing, but often with no clear idea why. Billboards exhorted people to "attend church this week," with no indication of which church or why. Politicians in their speeches regularly invoked God and affirmed that America was a God-fearing nation, but it was not always clear that they or their hearers fully understood what was necessary to be God-fearing.

The period 1945-1965 was a morally conservative time in American life. Traditional values were publicly honored and to a considerable extent lived by. (For example, after a predictable increase immediately after the War, the divorce rate actually began to decline.) This helped provide a stable environment, based on a broad moral consensus. It was a good time in which to raise children.

The less happy side of this moral conservatism was that it was often unthinking, merely habitual, and based on social custom.

When social customs began to change in the 1960s, many people found that they had no personal basis for continuing to live in accordance with their stated principles. They merely drifted with the tide. Furthermore, religion and traditional morality were closely identified with what came to be called "the establishment." When an anti-establishment mood hit the country, religious and moral values were among its first targets. Religion was viewed by many people not as something eternally true, to be adhered to through every vicissitude. It was merely a part of one's "life-style," perhaps appropriate to the 1950s but not to a changed society.

America after 1965 was indeed a changed society. Within a few years, it had probably changed as radically as it ever had in its long history. But it was the kind of change that was difficult to measure, and it was not as dramatic as the political and economic upheavals which interest historians. In essence, it was a transformation in the personal values and beliefs of countless Americans.

Perhaps surprisingly, the major cause of this change may well have been prosperity. From 1945 to at least 1975 most Americans experienced a constantly and perceptibly rising standard of living. Each year, almost every class of people, from the poor to the rich, found themselves at least a little better off then they had been the previous year. (Toward the end of the 1970s there were signs of a reversal of this trend, but the reversal was not yet dramatic. Most people were still better off than their parents had been.) The connection between prosperity and religious and moral decline ought not to be surprising to Christians. It has always been a Judaeo-Christian commonplace that when men prosper they tend to forget God. The Old Testament in particular makes this abundantly clear.

One of the weaknesses of the prevalent religiosity of the 1950s was the ease with which it accepted material prosperity. Relatively little thought was given to helping Christians cope with an economic success that might corrupt. Some preachers even equated prosperity with divine favor, a recurring temptation in the history of the church. For a long time there appeared no basic incompatibility between prosperity and fidelity. If anything, prosperity was seen as a way for devout Christians to give more money to the church or to charity.

But a subtle psychological process was taking place. More and more people were becoming accustomed to all their "needs" being met. At first these needs were really that. The Depression of the 1930s and the privations of the war years left many people close to poverty. But gradually "needs" came to be indistinguishable from "wants." Not only did people expect to have a car, they needed two, and then three. The annual vacation had to be taken at a comfortable resort. Every household had to get every new and expensive technological device, from kitchen equipment to large-screen televisions. Clothes were discarded merely because they were a bit out of style.

So long as this expectation of desire-fulfillment was confined to material goods it was dangerous to faith but not lethal. The graver troubles began when it was transferred to the spiritual and psychological planes as well. Put simply, Americans proved less and less able to accept any form of self-denial. They could not say no to themselves, and did not want others to say no to them either. Just as they took it as their birthright that they would eventually obtain all the goods they desired, so they began to take it as their birthright that they could do virtually anything they wanted with their lives.

The implications of this for personal morality were devastating. Spouses divorced, sometimes after years of marriage, because one or both parties found someone else who was more attractive and exciting. Pregnancies were aborted because they came at inconvenient times. People of all ages made free use of drugs merely to experience something new and thrilling.

This seemingly endless prosperity may also have inculcated in people a confidence in their own powers that was ultimately inimical to religion. Prosperity was the most tangible sign that "the system" was working. It was also experienced as a direct result of one's own hard work, talent, and dedication. The thought began to impress itself on people's minds that they could eventually get anything they wanted if only they wanted it badly enough, worked for it hard enough, and used their ingenuity.

The world was experienced as man's own creation. This left little room for God. Prosperous Americans of the 1960s and 1970s might continue to believe in God in some general way. They might even continue to call themselves Christians. But God's existence made little or no difference in their lives. They had little sense of sin and felt little need for redemption. God's commandments were regarded as, at best, guidelines, with each person devising his own morality in accordance with his conscience. People who thought they could obtain whatever they wanted through their own efforts saw little reason to pray and experienced little dependence on God. They had become Secular Humanists in practice, whatever they might call themselves.

This new secularity was also closely linked to social mobility, the opportunity to find a new place for oneself in society with greater prestige and material rewards. America has always been a country with great social mobility. It has no firmly established class system. It gives ample opportunity to men of talent and ambition. Throughout American history people have consistently found it possible to improve their lot by moving. Not only was this true in the days of the frontier, it is true today in a different way. For many people, advancement in a career involves willingness to move, and to move frequently.

Rapid, and even dramatic, upward mobility was a close corollary to the prosperity of the post-war period. Before the war, college graduates were still a rather rare minority. After the war, the proportion of high-school graduates attending college rapidly increased, until it reached nearly half in the early 1970s. During most of that period a college degree was practically a guarantee of economic opportunity. Millions of Americans who attended college were able to pursue goals which for their parents would have been utterly unrealistic.

This mobility reinforced the sense of self-reliance already alluded to. It also inculcated in people a sense of the necessity of "hanging loose," ready to move in whatever direction opportunity might call. American industry after World War II practiced a system of "planned obsolescence," whereby consumer products, machinery, styles, and many other things were expected to be discarded after a few years, to be replaced by something new. People became used to expecting that they would discard their old possessions periodically and replace them with models that were brighter and more modern.

Both things together—social mobility and planned obsolescence—created a mentality in which fixed beliefs, unchanging fidelities, and eternal truths came to seem like liabilities restricting movement and change. The person with the fewest commitments—marital, religious, moral, institutional, intellectual—was the person best able to take advantage of all the opportunities which society offered.

If America was still a predominantly religious society in the early 1960s, it went through a secularization process which was amazingly rapid. The process is not complete by any means. In some ways America remains a very religious nation. But common attitudes, and especially the kinds of attitudes which are regarded as respectable, underwent a swift change between 1965 and 1970. Although it was perhaps only a minority who were most affected, they were the trend-setters. They either had little interest in religion or were hostile to it. They either rejected traditional morality or were willing to compromise it endlessly. They contrived to place traditional religious belief on the permanent defensive.

FIVE

The Cult of Self-Worship

OSTENSIBLY, the 1960s were a time of disinterested idealism. Americans seemed to manifest a remarkable willingness to attack the most glaring problems of their society and to do so in a spirit of moral dedication. To an extent, this was indeed the case. But, less noticed at the time, a certain arrogant complacency underlay this idealism.

The early 1960s were the years of President John F. Kennedy, who inspired much of the idealism, orchestrated it, and directed it. The spirit of those years was one of pragmatic omnicompetence. The President himself seemed to symbolize a belief that Americans could do anything if they put their minds to it. The Kennedy years were marked by tremendous respect for intelligence, pragmatic skill, and cool self-reliance. All problems would be solved if approached correctly.

This spirit was not overtly secular, and the leading figures of the time, from Kennedy down, were at least nominal believers. It was, however, a spirit in which there was not much room for God, prayer, or obedience to divine law. Rarely in history did men have such a keen sense of their total dependence on their own ingenuity. In such circumstances, religion was merely a courtesy occasionally extended to God, much in the way that one might take time out from a busy schedule to visit an elderly grandparent.

Religiously the period achieved its most appropriate expression in an extremely influential book called *The Secular City* by an at least nominally Baptist theologian, Harvey Cox.

John Fitzgerald Kennedy (1917-63) was the first Roman Catholic president of the United States. In retrospect, however, it appears that Kennedy's religion did not penetrate very deeply into his personality, and he exemplified the pragmatic secularism of the early 1960s. While running for president he said in a speech that "whatever one's religion in private life may be, for the office-holder nothing can take precedence over his oath to uphold the Constitution and all its parts—including the First Amendment and the strict separation of church and state." Such statements gave rise to a tendency on the part of other politicians, Protestant as well as Catholic, to ignore religious considerations once in office, as though the Constitution requires that public officials be secularists. In practice, many politicians tend to deny religious values any meaningful role in public life.

Cox enthusiastically celebrated the spirit of pragmatism and secularity. While continuing to affirm God's existence and his ultimate authority in the affairs of men, Cox came close, on the practical level, to saying that God did not really matter. Man's religious obligation was to cultivate his talents and his dedication to making a better world. Specifically religious concerns, including prayer, could easily become "distractions" from this responsibility. In effect, Cox told believers to live as Secular Humanists and let religion take care of itself. It was a message which many Christians were eager to hear.

As could have been predicted, the high hopes and idealism of the Kennedy years were soon disappointed, not only because of the young President's assassination. His successor, Lyndon Johnson, in fact, carried on his programs, and with greater success than Kennedy had himself. But the dream of eradicating poverty and injustice from American life was not realized. There were many reasons for this—among them the Vietnam War, which divided the nation to its very core and diverted attention from domestic social problems. To some degree, that war explains the failure of the political dreams of the 1960s, but it too was the result of the same spirit of complacent, often arrogant self-reliance which the Kennedy years had generated. Political and military leaders persisted in thinking that just one more dose of American technical skill and personal determination would bring the war to an end.

By the middle of the 1960s, some segments of the nation, especially the young on college campuses, were in open revolt against "the system," a condition which would continue until the early 1970s and leave lasting marks on American society. Ostensibly, the reasons for the revolt were political: disappointment at the failure to realize the dreams of the Kennedy years, opposition to the war. However, almost as soon as the student rebellion began at the University of California at Berkeley in 1964, the Free Speech Movement, which was essentially political, was joined by the Filthy Speech Movement, which was not political at all although it pretended to be.

The young people who organized the campus revolts of the

1960s were the products of the "baby boom," the unusually large number of children born in the United States from the end of World War II through the 1950s. They were a highly self-conscious group which recognized the power of its numbers. Certain things, in particular rock music and films, had formed a distinctive youth culture which was at odds with the values of the parents' generation.

It was also the generation which had benefitted most from post-war prosperity. The parents had experienced the hard times before 1945 and had worked to improve their lot afterwards. Most of the young had no memory of hardship and accepted prosperity as their due. Their very status as college students was a form of privilege, freeing them for a prolonged period (often years beyond the standard undergraduate program) in which they had no social responsibilities. They were encouraged to explore themselves, their "needs," and the society around them, with a view to transforming it in accordance with their own vision.

The protests of the young against war, poverty, racism, and other undeniable social evils was, in part, motivated by genuinely outraged idealism. It was, in that sense, a credit to their sincerity. It was also partly the reaction of a generation which had always gotten what it wanted. "How dare the world not conform to my expectations" was, in effect, the cry of many. These young people had a low tolerance for frustration, and their rebellion was a collective demand that their parents' generation alleviate their frustration.

As already noted, the frustration was not only political. Before long it extended to things which were essentially self-indulgent and self-gratifying. All of these were put forth as "rights" on the same level of importance as political rights. The Filthy Speech Movement, which claimed the "right" to use in public words which had traditionally been banned from polite society and which were deeply offensive to many people, began the trend. Drugs became an integral part of the youth culture. Many young rebels were soon far more resentful of attempts to suppress drug use than they were of anything which might be

Harvey Cox of Harvard Divinity School, one of the most influential present-day Protestant theologians, illustrates the way in which a practical kind of secularism is not limited to professed nonbelievers. Religious liberals like Cox have demanded that the churches allow their "agenda" to be set for them by the secular world. In his most influential book, *The Secular City*, Cox wrote, "We do not speak to him [our neighbor] of God by trying to make him religious but, on the contrary, by encouraging him to come fully of age, putting away childish things." Among "childish things," Cox made clear, were many of the traditional beliefs and practices of Christianity.

happening in Vietnam. In "freedom marches" in the South, on college campuses, everywhere that the youth culture gathered in force—sexual "liberation" was also asserted as a basic right. Theorists of the movement articulated ambitious manifestoes explaining chastity as part of a system of political oppression. "Make love, not war" became the key slogan.

Young people had first pitted themselves against political institutions which they had come to regard as illegitimate. They refused to be drafted into the armed forces, disrupted work at campus institutes connected to the military, and prevented "reactionary" speakers from being heard. From there it was not very far to developing a visceral sense that all forms of established authority, all rules, all demands for obedience, were inherently illegitimate. The same government which wanted young people to fight in what they considered an immoral war also refused to let them use drugs. The same college authorities who cooperated with an immoral government forbade students to make love in the dormitories. The same parents who had, allegedly, acquiesced in an unjust society tried to impose hypocritical rules on their children.

What emerged from all this was a simple, only half-conscious principle of thought and behavior: "Whatever or whoever tries to tell me what to do is oppressing me. Any law, any institution, any figure of authority which I have not created myself is my enemy, an unjust oppressor of my liberty."

The political rebellion of the young collapsed fairly quickly. First, disinterested moral crusades, such as on behalf of poor blacks, were abandoned in favor of a preoccupation with the war. There the self-interest of the rebels was directly at stake. When the war ended, or when most of the educated middle-class young had found ways of avoiding the draft, the spirit of revolt shifted entirely to matters of self-gratification. On college campuses in particular a near-total revolution was effected in the course of less than one academic generation—four years. Not only did students, in effect, gain the right to cohabit in the dormitories and to use drugs, almost all rules pertaining to personal behavior were abolished. On many campuses faculty and administrators succumbed to student pressure to do away with almost all academic requirements as well. Education came to be regarded as wholly a matter of the student's subjective preference, one more expression of the sovereign ego.

It was presented at first as a conflict between generations. ("Don't trust anybody over thirty.") However, the youth rebellion would never have succeeded except that it always had important allies and sympathizers in the older generation— professors, journalists, clergy, some parents, even a few politicians. There were various motives for this sympathy. Some had a sincere admiration for the moral idealism and shared a political outlook. It is also obvious in retrospect that some adults responded enthusiastically to the youth rebellion from a desire to share in that rebellion vicariously. Many older people admitted that they had lived "uptight" lives and that they wanted to experience the same "liberation" that the young claimed for themselves.

There was irony. The young had been scathing in their condemnation of the materialism and self-indulgence of their parents. Some young people did sincerely try to live simple, frugal, even ascetic lives, although most of these experiments were of brief duration. The young rebels could think of themselves as unmaterialistic simply because their materialism took different forms from their parents'. Instead of cars they wanted motorcycles; instead of dish washers, stereos; instead of liquor, drugs. Their whole way of life—not only their possessions, but their freedom from social responsibility and the luxury of remaining a "student" endlessly—was made possible by the materialistic society they despised.

The expectation of self-satisfaction had been bred into the young from an early age by indulgent and affluent parents, who for years had not denied themselves many things. When the youth rebellion erupted, most parents were living a compromise between material self-indulgence and moral self-control. It was apparently possible to have all desired material goods while adhering to traditional moral and social constraints. Things had been slowly changing, however. From about 1960 on, for example, the divorce rate rose rapidly, after a decline in the previous decade. It was inevitable that a society to which everything material was "owed" should ultimately refuse to be bound by inconvenient moral restraints.

The example of the young, as many older people publicly admitted, was crucial. The 1970s was one of the few times in history when the older generation looked to the younger for guidance on how to live, rather than the reverse. At first disapproving, then intrigued, then sympathetic, finally thrilled, many parents began to emulate the "courage" of their offspring in throwing off all conventions. The young had snapped certain psychological bonds, and the vibrations of that snap struck responsive chords in their parents' psyches as well.

There were, of course, a variety of parental responses. Some of the older generation remained strongly disapproving of what the youth culture had wrought, and heartbroken when it affected their own children. Probably most parents were driven to an acceptance of the inevitable. It seemed as though every social force had conspired to make it impossible to bring up children according to the values the parents believed in. They learned to live with situations they would previously have found intolerable. Others, however, welcomed the assault on traditional values which the young had spearheaded. Where they did not join in the attack themselves, they were willing to enjoy its fruits, or to applaud the attackers.

The 1970s came to be called the "me decade." In official lore this supposedly marked a shift from the political idealism of the 1960s, but that "idealism" had always been in large measure self-interested. Where it did not involve direct self-interest, as in military conscription, it always involved an attitude of rejecting hated authority. Official lore also holds that the frequently narcissistic preoccupations of the 1970s were the result of disappointed political hopes; veterans of the battles of the 1960s turned "inward" because of the wounding of their political idealism. There was, however, a straight line from the self-interested idealism of one decade to the private concerns of the next. The thread (or heavy cable) that connected was a determination to throw off all constraints imposed from the outside on a wholly free self.

This attitude was secular in a most thorough and unrelenting way. For one thing, it was secular in a literal, etymological sense—a disdain for the past, often an unconcern for the future, a determination to live only for the moment. It was also secular in that it repudiated all moral rules and all spiritual authority. It often systematically violated many of those laws which Christianity claimed were God-given. Finally, it was secular in that anything "imposed" from the outside was regarded as an invasion of the self. This view of life leaves no room whatever for God in the lives of his creatures.

The gradual spread of the attitudes of the "me generation" are easy to trace. They appeared in the divorce statistics, the abortion statistics, the growing use of drugs even by respectable middle-aged people, the increasingly open and bitter antagonism to traditional values expressed in the media, and the seemingly large class of people who constitute an audience for everything morally iconoclastic.

Hardly anyone was immune. Those who did not completely accept the new world-view nonetheless often found themselves accepting parts of it, and being tolerant of most of it. Many people who still held traditional values in their own lives nonetheless were at pains not to be perceived as disapproving or "narrow." Often they gave up expecting to be able to form their children in those same values.

One obvious result of all this was the breakdown of families, which by the end of the 1970s had reached epidemic proportions. In some parts of the country the number of divorces equaled the number of marriages. Countless children are now raised by a single parent, or find themselves torn between two estranged parents. In over half of all households both parents work outside the home, so that even small children have only limited contact with their parents. Their upbringing has been taken over to a great extent by professionals. Increasing numbers of young people do not bother to get married at all. They live together on an informal basis, with the expectation that they will drift apart. The ideal of permanent commitment is now honored more in the breach than in the observance, and is often scoffed at. Many married people have decided not to have children, or to limit themselves to one or two.

The breakup of a marriage is often the result of tragic circumstances which the people involved have tried to avert. The alarming increase in recent years, however, is directly traceable to a softening of attitudes about things like commitment, fidelity, and love itself. What the culture of the 1970s taught many people was to place themselves first in any relationship and to be unwilling to make even minimal sacrifices for the sake of others. Marriages are entered into with the expectation that they will eventually fail. Children are regarded as a burden, to be avoided or thrown onto others. People take it as their basic right to "fulfill" themselves, no matter how damaging this may be to others. Many marriages now fail because one or both partners begin to look for greater excitement elsewhere.

Almost everyone has been affected by this spirit of self-indulgence. There is, in effect, a great conspiracy in America to extend toleration to all forms of questionable behavior as a way of insuring toleration for one's own. Homosexuality is a case in point. Many people now espouse the cause of "gay rights" because they realize that a society which approves of homosexuality will not disapprove of very many things. Even those who live in accordance with strict moral principles often find it necessary to be publicly tolerant of behavior of which they disapprove. There is no worse social stigma than being thought censorious or puritanical.

The 1970s were also the "me decade" in that never before in history was there more preoccupation with self-exploration, self-discovery, self-fulfillment. In earlier decades, a relatively few people, mainly the affluent, had consulted psychiatrists to overcome their personal problems. The practice was generally regarded as rather bizarre and as unnecessary for healthy people. By 1970, however, professional or pseudo-professional psychiatric help had become available to almost anybody who sought it. Increasing numbers of people did. Seeking such help was no longer a sign of lack of health, however. Instead, people began delving into their psyches, under direction, as a way of answering questions like "Who am I?", "How should I live?", "What can I believe in?", "How can I relate to others?" Before long these questions extended to "How can I be successful and assertive in life?" and "How can I get people to do what I want them to?"

On the foundation of such questions there arose a new American industry, comprehensively called the "human potential movement." Dozens of schools of thought, therapeutic techniques, and disciplinary regimens offered the key to realizing one's potential, getting in touch with one's feelings, overcoming obstacles to growth, etc. Some of the leaders of these movements were competent professionals, even if their values were often questionable. Others were of dubious integrity. Some could be called outright charlatans. Nonetheless they did an enormous business. Americans spent millions of dollars and countless hours attending seminars and workshops, reading books, listening to tapes—all designed to enable them to know themselves as never before.

Physically healthy people who persist in frequenting physicians are generally considered neurotic, possibly with too much money and not enough responsibility. During the 1970s, Americans in large numbers started to seek psychological help even when they had no mental problems in the customary sense of the term. This too was an important flowering of the culture of affluence. Many people, little by little, had come to believe that they owed themselves a perfectly fulfilled life. Having satisfied so many of their material desires, they had now come to expect spiritual fulfillment as well. Earlier generations of dissatisfied materialists often turned to religion or to humanitarian service to bring meaning to their lives. This generation decided to probe ever more deeply into themselves. They turned the state of their pysches into the principal preoccupation of their existence.

This attitude is profoundly secular and inherently irreligious.

Even nonbelievers noted its pathology, like the historian Christopher Lasch in his book, *The Culture of Narcissism.* Preoccupation with the self became, for many people, a virtual obsession with it. They began spending most of their waking hours pondering ways of improving their personalities and discovering how to get more out of life. This narcissism was both physical and psychological. The American obsession with diet and exercise, while commendable from the point of view of health, has been mainly motivated by a kind of worship of one's own body.

Only a small minority of people actually participated in encounter groups, transactional analysis, est seminars, or the host of other programs which offered freedom from personal constraint. But the attitudes disseminated in these programs spread everywhere in the culture and were picked up, often half-consciously, by people who had no idea where they came from. The distinguishing characteristic of the new narcissism was precisely an unhealthy, almost obsessive, interest in the self. It was marked by the assumptions that one's personal emotional well-being is the greatest good in life, that most of the time the self is entitled to get whatever it wants, that restraints on those desires are almost always unjust and unhealthy, and that "feeling good" about something is the highest test of whether that thing is legitimate. These attitudes have infected even many Christians, who do not realize how deeply they have drunk of a pagan concoction.

The psychologist Paul Vitz, in his book *Psychology as Religion,* has traced some of the philosophical roots of this movement. Most of those roots go back to what is broadly termed Humanistic Psychology, including such leading thinkers as Eric Fromm, Carl Rogers, and Abraham Maslow.

The term Humanistic Psychology is not used to imply godlessness. Rather it is intended to distinguish it from certain other schools of psychology, such as Freudianism and modern behaviorism. The humanistic psychologists lay heavy stress on human freedom and on the capacity of human nature for growth and improvement; the classical psychological tradition stem-

Erich Fromm is one of the most popular contemporary psychologists. His "humanistic psychology" has attracted many religious believers because it seems to provide a hopeful alternative to the behaviorism of men like B.F. Skinner (see Chapter 9). However, Fromm's humanism not only refers to the value he places on man but also to his effective denial of God. Fromm cannot respect religion in the terms in which believers profess it. Like Freud, he regards it as an illusion. Typical of his approach to faith is his interpretation of the early Christians' beliefs concerning Jesus: "Consciously they did not dare to slander the fatherly God. . . . But the unconscious hostility to the divine father found expression in the Christ fantasy. . . . The belief in the elevation of a man to god was thus the expression of an unconscious wish for the removal of the divine father."

ming from Freud tends to make man the result of certain impersonal biological and psychological forces over which he has little control.

The humanistic psychologists have corrected the sometimes excessive pessimism and narrowness of classical psychology. In some ways their work is more easily reconciled with Christianity than is Freud's. For this reason, it has had great appeal in religious circles. However, Vitz points out that it finally rests on foundations which are incompatible with Christian faith. It has no realization of sin, so that practically all human impulses are treated as good. Evil is usually dismissed merely as "failure to grow," or as the unfortunate result of psychological "repressions" of various kinds. Although it aims to point beyond mere selfishness, Humanistic Psychology encourages selfishness at least at an intermediate stage. There is no real appreciation of the Christian ideal of selfless love. Humanistic Psychology is also inherently relativistic where moral and spiritual values are concerned. It encourages people to choose or create their own values and to resist those "imposed" on them by others, including religion. Several of the leading humanistic psychologists (Rogers and Fromm, for example) are quite hostile to orthodox religion.

Phrases like "Let it all hang out," "Do your own thing," "Get in touch with your feelings," "If it feels good, do it," "Don't lay a heavy trip on me" are now popular slogans of the psychological revolution. From a Christian perspective, these slogans and the philosophies which lie behind them fail to recognize man as a creature and child of God, standing under judgment. Man is to live not primarily to satisfy his own desires but to fulfill God's plan. Sinful tendencies are part of his nature. He must be fully aware of the treacherous character even of his apparently good impulses and must compensate for it by some kind of objective and authoritative spiritual guidance. Happiness and self-fulfillment are not, for the Christian, what the world means by those terms. Christ's paradox, "He who loses his life will save it," remains central.

Without fully realizing it, today's devotees of popular

psychology, including many people in the churches, have accepted Feuerbach's assertion that so long as God exists man can never be free. The aim of most popular psychology is to abolish all sense of God's objective existence, and especially all sense of the existence of an objective, divinely inspired moral law. Right and wrong are regarded as essentially relative to the "needs" of each individual, and practically anything can be justified according to those subjective needs. The determinedly modern man lives in constant terror that the old objective moral authority will once again intrude itself in his life. He spends a great deal of his time reacting against every vestige of that authority.

It is not clear that people today actually behave in a more sinful way than their ancestors did. What is undeniably different, however, is how they think about their sins. A skewed modern psychology not only recognizes neurotic guilt, which is real and a perversion of genuine moral sense, but equates all sense of sin with such guilt and defines it as sick. There is no longer the possibility of repentance, because the sin itself is rationalized, even proclaimed virtuous. Repentance is ruled out as a product of a neurotic guilt which stifles personal growth. Sins of the flesh, traditionally regarded in Christianity as the least serious because mostly the result of weakness rather than pride, have now been turned into sins of pride. The sinner wears his sin as a badge of honor, boasts of his emancipation from all moral authority, and, in effect, dares God to judge him.

The effects of this moral and psychological revolution are perhaps most easily seen in the way in which certain aspects of behavior relating to sex—divorce, adultery, abortion, homosexuality—have now been justified. Their practitioners defiantly demand that even the churches grant them a stamp of approval. However, the revolution goes deeper. It consists in a frank and unembarrassed selfishness which has not been respectable in the Western world since the days of Rome. It amounts to a repeal of the entire Christian ethic of unselfish love and self-denial in favor of an exhortation to follow one's impulses wherever they may lead. It is an attitude which has deep implications for family life, personal relationships, business, politics, and every other aspect of existence.

Thoughtful Humanists still draw on the reserves of two thousand years of Christian morality. They do not wish to bring about a barbaric world in which self-gratification is the only accepted motive for action. They assume that certain basic moral attitudes are so deeply ingrained in people that they will survive no matter what. Commonly they advise, in effect, "Do whatever you want so long as it doesn't hurt anybody." But the Christian realization of the inherent sinfulness of man means, among other things, a recognition of man's endless capacity for self-deception. People assure themselves they are not hurting others even when acts of aggression and injustice are necessary for them to get what they want. (Abortion is an obvious example. A woman can assert her "right" to an abortion only by denying the humanity of the unborn child.) Prevalent attitudes derived from popular psychology provide no basis for constructing a workable morality; they merely provide means for negating traditional morality.

Christians are sometimes criticized for emphasizing sexual behavior too much when they talk about morality, but for the most part that choice has been made for them over the past twenty years. The militant secularism of the 1970s chose sexuality as its chief point of conflict with Christian morality for a variety of reasons: the fact that it had a (quite literally) seductive appeal to many people, the fact that feelings of guilt and resentment could be most easily stirred up in that area, and the suspicion that it was there that the churches were most vulnerable.

It is important that Christians keep their moral priorities straight and not fall into the trap of thinking that sex is everything. It is also the case that sexuality, now the symbol of the new "liberation," cannot be ignored. The attack on traditional sexual morality was successful to the extent that traditional morals rested not on firmly held principles but on custom and social convention. When respect for convention and respectability crumbled, morality went with it, except for people with a highly developed moral code rooted in conscious religious beliefs. The attack on the family is a close correlative of the sexual revolution, because the family is seen as the bastion of respectability and the agency through which traditional values are inculcated in children.

The moral revolution of the past twenty years is, in one sense, the fulfillment of forces set in motion in the Enlightenment. The full implications were drawn out in the nineteenth century by Feuerbach and Nietzsche. But the revolution has turned out differently from what its progenitors expected in one way: it is not, for the most part, openly and officially atheistic. This fact, however, should be of only very limited comfort to believers. Old-style atheists paid God the compliment of taking him seriously. They had to deny him because they recognized how completely he dominates man's life on earth. The children of contemporary culture, however, can live with God because they treat God merely as an idea they are free to play with in whatever way they see fit. In a sense, God is simply one more pleasure which they refuse to deny themselves.

Harvey Cox's *Secular City* could almost have been used as an argument for atheism. Although Cox did not intend it as such, it seemed to say that belief in God is unnecessary and even a dangerous distraction from life. Perhaps man would be better off without God. A few years later, Cox published *The Seduction of the Spirit*. Someone sarcastically said it might have been subtitled "*Playboy*'s Guide to Religion in the 1970s." Cox told his readers that religion could be fun. More precisely he told them that there are all sorts of gratifying experiences to be gotten out of religion, if only people know where to look for them and how to exploit them. The trick, according to Cox, is not to believe in the teachings of the various world religions as those religions proclaim them. The religious man of the late twentieth century is someone "open" to practically every religious practice or discipline, but only to the degree that they seem to enhance his subjective sense of well-being. Whereas practically all the religions of the world have demanded that the individual submit himself to something greater than himself,

Cox reverses the process. The individual becomes the final test of everything, and all religion is subordinated to the authority of the self seeking infinite gratification.

During the pragmatic, hardheaded Kennedy era, most educated people would have laughed at things like astrology, witchcraft, and nature-worship and would have proclaimed religions like Zen Buddhism at best irrelevant to life in the industrialized West. Yet by the end of the 1960s, these and many others had gained a totally unexpected respectability. The 1970s were not secular in the sense that they were an overtly non-religious period. They were, if anything, a kind of religious greenhouse, in which every kind of exotic plant bloomed.

This flowering should not be dismissed totally, since it is in part a testimony to the inherently religious character of human nature. Religion cannot be suppressed forever. If suppressed, it comes back, sometimes in bizarre and deformed ways. The religiosity of the 1970s was undoubtedly also a reflection of the spiritual confusion and alienation of so many alumni of the previous decade. Having wantonly thrown away whatever beliefs they had grown up with, they now found a need to believe in something.

Thus there emerged a catalogue of religious or pseudo-religious movements which rivalled the catalogue of psychological movements promising self-fulfillment: Zen, American Indian religions, astrology, Hinduism, witchcraft and magic, numerous schools of meditation, Hare Krishna, Rev. Moon's Unification Church, etc. What all these had in common was a hunger for the spiritual in life, but the problem, from the Christian perspective, was precisely there. One of most neglected of Christ's sayings is "You have not chosen me; I have chosen you." The desire for God has always played an important role in the conversion of people to Christ. In itself this hunger is not enough. By itself it easily perverts genuine religion.

Many of the people who turned to religion in the 1970s were merely advancing one step farther along the road which their egotism had opened up to them. Just as they expected all their material wants to be taken care of, just as they heedlessly threw off all social and moral constraints which they found inconvenient, so they had come to expect that their spiritual "needs" would also be fulfilled. In a sense, they decided that religion was too delicious to waste on believers. Why could not the nonbeliever also enjoy the delights of mystical experience (often now drug-induced), join in dramatic and mysterious rituals from the East, conjure up a comforting spiritual presence to assure him that he is not alone in a cold universe?

Virtually all Christians have sought gratification of one kind or another from their religion. Among its promises is the promise of ultimate happiness. But, true Christians have always realized that the comforts of faith are finally the fruits of obedience. The newly enthusiastic devotees of the popular religion refused to render such. The religious traditions of the world were to them like a marvellous tree laden with ripe fruits. They were free to pick and enjoy whatever fruits struck their fancy, to leave those that seemed slightly bitter, and above all never to worry where the tree came from or how it was nourished and maintained.

The older secularism was hostile to religion and sought to destroy it. The newer secularism often now destroys the soul of religion while keeping its body. In the end, while this may offer the prospect of reconverting the skeptic to genuine faith, it also renders that task a great deal harder. The skeptic has learned to pervert almost every aspect of religion to his own uses.

SIX

The Mass Media

ANTI-RELIGIOUS SENTIMENT in earlier times was mostly
confined to elite circles. Print was virtually the only means
by which new ideas were disseminated, and the great majority
of people, until at least the middle of the nineteenth century,
were illiterate. It is the mass media which, more than anything
else, account for the rapid spread of secularism in the late
twentieth century.

For a long time, the media were not in principle biased
towards secular values. If anything, the opposite seemed to be
the case. While radical ideas were discussed in somewhat
rarified social settings, in popular culture traditional values
were still honored. American films are an example. There was a
brief flurry of experimentation with "daring" themes around
1930. The popular outcry was so strong that the film industry
introduced voluntary censorship, which remained in effect for
over thirty years. During that time, no matter how objectionable
certain scenes in certain films might be, there was a generally
accepted code whereby virtue had to be honored (and usually
rewarded), while vice had to be acknowledged as such (and
usually punished). Moral and religious values were never
ridiculed or attacked.

As did so many other things, the mass media began to change
around 1965, with the most dramatic changes occurring during
the 1970s. The changes were related to the pervasive prosperity
of the period, and to the cult of self-worship which this
produced. Put simply, those who controlled the media realized

that there was a substantial audience which had broken with traditional moral values and wanted entertainment that ventured into forbidden territory in hitherto forbidden ways. Not only were taboo subjects treated, they were treated iconoclastically; traditional moral values were ridiculed, assaulted, and ground into dust. The audience for this kind of entertainment wanted to experience the thrill of the forbidden. It also sought confirmation that its own break with the past was justified. Insecure in their rebellion at the deepest level of their personalities, they needed repeated public assaults on those values as a means of reassurance.

But if the revolution in the media had been supported solely by self-conscious moral rebels, its scope would have been far narrower. The manipulators of the media also suspected, correctly as it turned out, that many people who professed traditional values would nonetheless accept the new iconoclasm simply as entertainment, without examining too closely the values behind it. The moral corruption which affected even many good people in America was nowhere more ruthlessly revealed than here. As part of the general spirit of self-gratification, many people began to feel, instinctively and often without fully realizing it, that one of the things they "owed" themselves was a constant diet of entertainment. When the media underwent their moral revolution during the 1970s, many professedly Christian people made no protest. In fact, they remained an enthusiastic part of the audience because they found the new fare diverting. They drew an impregnable line between their religious lives and the hours they spent relaxing, convinced that what they consumed as entertainment could not affect their personal values.

In a great many instances, this belief was naive. Many people were corrupted through means they did not take seriously. Where parents proved relatively immune, children did not. Above all, even where there was some immunity, many Christians made the moral revolution in the media possible because they patronized it. In effect, they helped to subsidize the corruption of others.

This moral revolution was achieved in a variety of ways. On the simplest level, it consisted merely of talking about what was hitherto unmentionable. Subjects previously forbidden in the popular media (abortion, incest) were presented for the first time. In the beginning these presentations were brief, cautious, blandly neutral. There were cries of protest. These were met by boasts about how "tastefully" the subject had been dealt with. "After all," the argument ran, "knowledge is better than ignorance. No one can object to the public recognition that certain things exist. In the end, we will all be better off for our frank willingness to talk about our problems."

There were many flaws in this argument. Among them is the general unsuitability of the mass media for a serious discussion of sensitive and delicate issues of any kind. By their very nature, the media deal with such questions briefly, simplistically, and in a style which borders on the sensational. Their aim is not primarily to explore problems responsibly but to attract the largest possible audience. Since the various media are in competition with each other, there is strong pressure on each to do something just a bit more "daring" than its competitors.

The mass media also have the power to confer instant respectability. In a mass society, to be ignored is the worst possible fate. To be noticed is tantamount to being deemed worthy. To be noticed by a mass audience is almost a kind of canonization. No matter how seemingly "neutral" the treatment, when certain ideas are given time and space in the media they acquire a respectability that increases with frequency. Then comes the point where previously taboo subjects become familiar and acceptable. There is deep hypocrisy in the media's pious claims that they merely reflect reality and do not shape it. In fact the power of celebrity is used deliberately and selectively in order to effect changes in values.

The second stage of the revolution is ridicule, the single most powerful weapon in any attempt to discredit accepted beliefs. Within a remarkably brief time, values the media had celebrated during the 1950s (family, religion, patriotism) were subjected to a merciless and constant barrage of satire. Only people with an exceptionally strong commitment to their beliefs could withstand being depicted as ignorant buffoons. Countless Christians subtly adjusted their beliefs, or at least the way in which they presented those beliefs to the public, in order to avoid ridicule. Negative stereotypes were created, and people who believed in traditional values were kept busy avoiding being trapped in those stereotypes.

The final stage of the moral revolution is the media's exploitation of traditional American sympathy for the underdog. Judaeo-Christian morality, although eroding for a long time and on the defensive almost everywhere in the Western world, is presented as a powerful, dominant, and even tyrannical system against which only a few brave souls make a heroic stand on behalf of freedom. Thus secularists of all kinds and those who deny traditional morality in words and behavior are treated as heroes by the media. Their stories are told over and over again in order to elicit sympathy and, finally, agreement.

Probably the greatest power which the mass media possess is the ability, in effect, to define reality. What is presented in the media, and the way in which it is presented, are for many people the equivalent of what is real. By determining what ideas will be discussed in public, the media determine which ideas are to be considered respectable, rational, and true. Those excluded from discussion, or treated only in a negative way, are conversely defined as disreputable, irrational, and false.

The media have the power almost to confer existence itself. Unless a belief or an institution receives some recognition, it does not exist. Even those who know that the media are fundamentally hostile to their values nonetheless court media recognition as a way of achieving status in the public eye.

Many people also look to the media for authoritative guidance in their own lives, especially when traditional sources of authority—family, church, school—are in decline. From the media, people learn how to dress, what to eat and drink, and what kind of car to drive. They also learn how they should think about public issues, how they should react to personal crises, how they should live their lives. The rapid spread of the ideology of Women's Liberation, for example, is in large measure due to the overwhelming sympathy of the media towards that movement. American women are invited to define themselves by reference to models the media hold up to them. Deviation from those models (being "just a housewife," for example) is embarrassing and even reprehensible.

The media's secularism should be recognized in its fullness. Complaints about television, in particular, have tended to focus on the twin problems of sex and violence, but the nature of the sickness goes a good deal deeper. It is directly related to the social circumstances which made the revolution in values possible in the first place.

For the most part, the media depend on advertising for their support; it is key to their profit. To an extent, therefore, the media must appeal to the widest possible audience. Roughly, the larger the audience, the more advertising and the greater profit.

But it is not quite that simple. If it were, the secularization process would not have been so swift and so complete. All opinion polls show the great majority of Americans wedded to traditional moral and religious values, despite some erosion over the past twenty years. However, as noted, many religious believers have at least passively supported the media's moral revolution by their complete separation of entertainment from other areas of their lives.

Advertising is not directed simply at the greatest number of people, but rather at the greatest number of potential buyers of the advertised product. Certain commodities are bought by practically everybody, but many items are available only to a limited class of people. Many advertisers are primarily interested in an elite market—people who have money and are likely to spend it.

In general, older, more traditional people have had a lifetime in which to accumulate savings and make investments. If retired, they also have the leisure to buy and enjoy things they may have denied themselves in earlier years. But other aspects of aging tend to cancel this out—illness, weariness, a traditional frugality, the desire to live simply in one's declining years. On the other hand, younger people raising families do not possess a great deal of "disposable income," money left over after the necessities. The shopping habits of young parents are likely to be determined by very practical considerations.

By the 1970s, a recognizable new class had emerged—people young enough to be active and mobile, but old enough to have accumulated a certain amount of wealth, above average in income, and bound by a minimum of family responsibilities.

The "typical" example of such people in contemporary society is the couple (married or unmarried) with one child or none and no desire to increase that number. They are educated professional people or are lucratively employed in business. They have taken maximum advantage of the new prosperity, and their entire outlook on life is shaped by that prosperity. Such people want only "the best" for themselves, not only in material goods but also in their way of life. They have made themselves maximally mobile. They are prepared to move— geographically, spiritually, intellectually, in terms of career—in whatever direction seems to offer the greatest and most gratifying opportunities.

Such people have more or less consciously chosen to sacrifice the joys and responsibilities of children for the sake of their own gratification. If they have children they arrange for them to be raised to a great extent by other people. Two incomes are essential to their way of life. They have the greatest possible "disposable income," and are the advertisers' favored target.

Such people are likely to be highly secular in their outlook. If they belong to a church (they probably do not), it is a liberal church peopled mainly by others like themselves. Their way of life would be difficult to reconcile with traditional religious and moral values, and the rejection of those values is a pre-condition for living the way they do.

Certain of the media (for example, *Playboy* magazine) are aimed almost exclusively at such people. They are the people who buy luxury cars, designer clothes, and condominiums. They patronize exclusive restaurants, stock their cellars with fine wines, and travel all over the world for vacations or business. Even in those media (for example, television networks) which reach a wider audience, such "preferred customers" have a disproportionate influence.

The media began their moral revolution secure in the belief that, whatever popular outcry might ensue, they were unlikely to alienate those they most wanted to reach. Indeed, many such people were eager for more "sophisticated" entertainment. They were in principle "open to all points of view" and were anxious to see "controversial" subjects explored "frankly." These are people who must eventually shatter all taboos because they deny themselves nothing. Their taste in "sophisticated" entertainment reinforces their self-image, and they are estranged from traditional moral values.

An overlooked cause of the moral revolution is also the style of life of many media people themselves. For whatever reason—the pressures of their work, the unreality of the media world, or because the entertainment profession attracts iconoclastic people to begin with—it appears that there are few moral traditionalists in the industry. In his book *The View from Sunset Boulevard,* Ben Stein interviewed television producers and writers. He found, overwhelmingly, that they are not only devotees of "the new morality"; they think traditional religion and morality are meaningless or even pernicious.

Thus the personal values of media people in conjunction with the personal values of their favored audience promote a particular point of view at odds with the expressed values of a majority of Americans. This is one of the places where the hypocrisy of media people is most blatant. They tend to treat all criticism as a threat to freedom of expression and wrap themselves in a high-minded moral rhetoric. Yet profit is almost their sole purpose for existence. A small and unrepresentative group of people imposes its skewed view of reality on everyone else.

The essence of the media's secularism is self-worship. Implicitly denying the existence of God or an objective moral order, they reduce life to an endless quest for personal fulfillment. Anything which some people find "meaningful" automatically acquires legitimacy, provided it runs counter to traditional beliefs. Life is depicted as a process which demands constant acts of rebellion against all moral absolutes and all social rules. The "free" individual is regarded as the one who has thrown off all constraints of any kind—religious, moral, familial, cultural, political—in order to make repeated assertions of "liberation" from all authority.

This kind of freedom is endlessly celebrated in the media, its devotees the new American heroes. This canonization also stimulates the sales which make advertising possible. There is a deep connection between this secular amorality and certain features of the American economy, in which total personal mobility is a requisite both for one's job and for being the best possible consumer.

By their very nature, the mass media are incapable of dealing with permanent truths, much less with the things of eternity. Newspapers are made to be thrown away the next day. The television image is gone almost instantly. Very few films are ever seen a second time. The media are constructed so as to deal with what is ephemeral, insubstantial, even illusory. It is of their essence that what is celebrated one year is denigrated or ignored the next. Regardless of explicit content, one of the most important messages the media convey to people is that change is the only reliable rule of life. In order to exist comfortably in the modern world it is necessary to hold only very loosely to one's beliefs and loyalties, because tomorrow the unrelenting demands of the culture will require a radical shift in those loyalties.

Each of the media function somewhat differently, even though each tends to the same result.

By far the most frankly pagan and anti-religious branch of mass culture, at least since the middle 1960s, is popular music. In no other branch is the depravity of the moral revolution more easily grasped. Traditionally the popular-music industry—from "Tin Pan Alley" of the early years of this century down to celebrities like Bing Crosby and Perry Como in the 1950s—

Elvis Presley, precisely because he proclaimed himself a believer in God, pointed up the deeply ingrained secularism of contemporary popular culture. Despite his often reassuring words and diffident manner, Presley's music and theatrical style had the effect of stimulating a kind of erotic rebellion among his followers. After his death it was revealed that, totally confused in mind, he had led a debauched life in which pleasure alone seemed to have had meaning.

reflected established moral and religious beliefs and, for the most part, supported them.

The first break came with the earliest rock singers of the 1950s, especially Elvis Presley. Presley was himself a proclaimed religious believer who told the public that he too lived according to Christian morality. But, as clearsighted observers noted even at the time, there was a contradiction between Presley's wholesome words and his suggestive actions. His theatrical style was aggressively erotic, frankly abandoned, and designed to arouse similar reactions in his audience. After his death, it was revealed that he was a deeply divided man, torn between moral ideals he sincerely believed in at some level of his being and a personal life totally debauched by drugs and sensual indulgence.

The revolution of rock music preceded the revolutions in other branches of the media and to a great extent made them possible. It was unique in being, perhaps, the only such revolution in which ideas were unimportant. The lyrics of songs were for a while unobjectionable. Not many people paid attention to them anyway. Rather, rock music assaulted people in a deeper, largely unconscious level of their being. It proclaimed in its rhythms and in the personal style of its devotees the annihilation of all moral restraint, hedonistic abandon, and ecstatic acting out of forbidden desires.

When the Beatles appeared in the middle 1960s they at first seemed merely boyish and playful. But as they grew more "serious" they revealed still other dimensions of the rock revolution. Precisely because they were less blatantly shocking than other groups (like the Rolling Stones), they could insinuate their iconoclastic energies in subtle, almost surgically precise ways. They were quickly elevated above the level of mere entertainers and came to be treated as prophets, sages, and moral heroes. They were mainly irreligious but could be overtly anti-religious. In the song "Eleanor Rigby," after describing a Christian funeral, they intone "No one was saved." Most importantly, they, more than perhaps anyone else, were responsible for elevating narcissistic self-absorption to the level of a cult, deifying personal and subjective feelings, and establishing self-satisfaction as the principal goal of existence.

By the 1970s, the rock-music industry had become openly nihilistic, its leading practitioners seemingly motivated by the desire to shock, affront, destroy, and negate. An Arizona minister's son appeared on stage in women's clothes, called himself Alice Cooper, and performed mock executions and suicides, which sometimes included the actual dismemberment of chickens. The Rolling Stones stirred up such frenzied passions in their followers that they took to hiring members of a motorcycle gang, The Hell's Angels, to protect them during concerts. (At one concert their bodyguards wantonly killed a young man who was approaching the performers on stage.) In costume, in lyrics, in their lives offstage, the leading rock stars of the 1970s degenerated into beings cut off from all spiritual roots, wholly self-absorbed, unrelentingly hedonistic, and often brutal. Yet their influence did not diminish. Two generations of young people all over the world were corrupted by them.

The economics of the rock-music industry is directly relevant to understanding this phenomenon. Popular music is only partly dependent on advertising (mainly through radio). It depends rather on direct purchase by the customer of records and concert tickets. The popularity of rock coincided with the emergence of the largest generation of young people in American history. These young people had always had their desires catered to and were the most affluent younger generation in history. Supported by their parents, they had a good deal of "disposable income."

The popular-music industry deliberately set out to create a youth culture which was highly self-conscious and at odds with the culture of the parents' generation. The new culture exploited the young's perennial restlessness under parental authority and their, quite literal, irresponsibility. Modern adolescents are kept in a condition of immaturity and are not held fully responsible for what they think or do. They are

The Rolling Stones deliberately cultivated a style and an image that might legitimately be called demonic. They systematically flouted every religious, moral, and social rule and stirred up in their admirers a pervasive spirit of nihilistic denial of every accepted belief, sometimes to the point of violence.

systematically encouraged to "find themselves." This makes for a strong sense of egotism and rebellion against all external constraints.

The youth culture has one thing in common with the more sophisticated culture of older iconoclasts. Neither, because of its alienation from family and religion, has much stake in the future, even less in the prospect of eternity. Both groups, for different reasons, live in an eternal present dedicated to self-satisfaction. Both are secularists in the most literal sense, wholly bound to the time in which they live.

The film industry during the past twenty years has followed a curve roughly parallel to that of the popular-music industry, although perhaps somewhat less sharp. In both cases, there has been a sudden and swift movement from moral conservatism to moral iconoclasm. In both cases the medium depends primarily not on advertising but on direct patronage by the consumer. In both cases the principal consumers are young people. The "family film" practically disappeared during the 1960s, probably the victim of television. Films came to be heavily patronized by young people who sought their entertainment outside the home. Films became "franker" and more "serious." Predictably, this seriousness was equated with the prejudices of the counterculture.

The size and influence of these branches of the media catering primarily to youth has wrought a special kind of revolution in American society. In the past, whatever youth culture existed—literature for young people, for example, or Walt Disney films—aimed to integrate youth into the values of the adult world. There was no contradiction between the content of the youth media and the beliefs of parents. They were merely different stages of development. Now, however, the youth culture is explicitly opposed to parental values, sets itself up as a rival authority, and seeks to prolong adolescent attitudes throughout life. The moral confusion of so many young adults can be traced directly to their previous immersion in a special youth culture from which they have never escaped.

If rock music was the catalyst which got the moral revolution started, television has been by far its chief disseminator. It would be almost impossible to overestimate its influence.

In some ways television remains the most cautious of the media. The limited number of channels makes government regulation necessary and makes television stations at least somewhat answerable to public opinion. But this relative caution is offset by the medium's immense range; it reaches almost every American.

Television is primarily an entertainment medium, and primarily a profit-making one. The economics of advertising is maximally operative. Prior to the 1960s, television entertainment was criticized as bland, boring, and lacking in substance. During the past twenty years there has been a deliberate effort to overcome this criticism. It is evidence both of the industry's lack of imagination and of its crudely stereotypic thinking that the only way writers and producers can make their programs more "meaningful" is by the now-familiar assaults on traditional values. A program gains a reputation for "seriousness" to the extent that it deals with hitherto taboo subjects. There is irresistible pressure towards the increasingly sensational.

The chief prophet of what might be called the "new television" was Norman Lear, creator of *All in the Family, Maude,* and *Mary Hartman.* Lear was praised for going beyond mere entertainment to give audiences "thoughtful" comedies. But his programs were mainly devices for disseminating his own ideology. *All in the Family,* the most popular, presented Archie Bunker as the quintessential ignorant bigot. Since Archie believed in God, country, family, and traditional sexual morality, those beliefs were tarred with the same brush. Obviously, no humane, thoughtful person could hold such beliefs. For contrast, Lear's programs also presented people who dissented from such values, models of rational humaneness.

The passive cooperation of religious believers in their own destruction was illustrated in the popularity of *All in the Family.* People accepted ideas in the guise of entertainment which they would have rejected indignantly had they been confronted with

Archie Bunker, played by Carroll O'Connor on the weekly program *All in the Family,* was one of the most popular figures in the history of television. The creation of the aggressive secularist producer Norman Lear, the program ridiculed traditional moral and religious beliefs, mainly by wrapping them together in the personality of Archie, who was portrayed as crude, ignorant, and bigoted. Such propaganda has been incessant in the mass media and reflects the way in which highly secularized media personnel view "straight" society, especially religion.

them outright. In 1980, Lear founded an organization with the arrogant title People for the American Way and sent out letters that almost hysterically denounced conservative religious movements as a threat to American freedom.

Lear's career is not the only example of blatant use of television for propaganda. The "talk shows," such as Phil Donahue's, compulsively seek out spokesmen for "controversial" ideas and actions. They rarely allow defenders of traditional values equal time. The daytime "soap operas," once the stronghold of genteel domesticity, have become display cases for every kind of depravity.

Just as destructive as its concentration on what is deviant and amoral has been television's general ignoring of religion as a positive force. Religious programs are usually confined to Sunday mornings, when the audience is small. Such programs are token concessions by stations required by law to give time for public service. When providing viewers with fictional images of what life is like, television rarely adverts to the fact that, for the great majority of Americans, religious belief is an integral part of their lives. Religiously motivated characters are likely to be neurotics for whom religion is a form of sickness. Rarely are sympathetic characters presented whose lives are strengthened by prayer or by the guidance of clergy. Millions of Americans attend church on Sunday and pray in their homes, but rarely are they shown doing this on television.

Television is also the society's principal disseminator of "news"—information about the world and, by implication, how to live in the world. Here religion sometimes fares better. It is not ignored as completely as it is in television entertainment. However, in keeping with its bias in favor of what is ephemeral and sensational, television news compulsively treats religion according to a single formula. That formula essentially consists in searching for religious factions in conflict with one another, one of which can be called "liberal," the other "conservative." The liberals are then treated as the voice of reason and compassion against the rigidity and irrationality of the defenders of religious orthodoxy. Often, by a judicious editing of film, liberals are presented at their best, conservatives at their worst. When Pope John Paul II appeared in America as a formidable spokesman for orthodoxy in 1979, the media effectively undercut his message by providing commentators each evening who dutifully pointed out the "errors" in the Pope's words. Television is especially eager to give time to church members who attack the Christian code of sexual ethics or who are partisans of Women's Liberation. Sometimes such people are, overnight, set up as heroes.

The behavior of the print media—newspapers and magazines—is not essentially different from that of television. There is a vast proliferation of journals of all kinds, many of them religious in nature. However, the major print media which reach mass audiences share in the general secularist prejudices of the other media. Because the print media can give more space to subjects, orthodox Christians probably get more attention there than they do on television. However, the standard way in which newspapers deal with religious questions is to devote the headlines and the opening paragraphs to dissenters and secularizers, so that only the most diligent readers reach the later paragraphs in which orthodoxy is allowed a token voice.

The mass media distort religion in a very fundamental way. Properly understood, religion is something which goes very deep in a person's being; it permeates all of existence. The media, however, tend to notice it only when it generates controversy. Furthermore, it must be controversy which is easily understood in secular terms—the "liberation" of women, for example, or sexual "freedom." The media allow people to view religion only as filtered through secularist lenses. Although the media piously insist that they merely seek to give expression to "unpopular" views, the effect of their revolution has been to give deviant ideas privileged status and to banish orthodoxy to the darkest corners.

There is no doubt that the media seek to dominate public opinion. For all their talk about freedom and diversity, there is remarkably little diversity among the media. By 1980, the attacks on Evangelicals like Jerry Falwell and Don Wildmon's

Coalition for Better Television had become frequently savage and hysterical. In no small measure this was due to fear that the long-standing secularist monopoly on communications was in danger of being broken.

An important development of the late 1970s was the emergence of wide-reaching religious telecasting, most of it under Evangelical Protestant auspices. Some Christians have legitimate questions about this development (for example, how substantial is a conversion gained over television?). The phenomenon has, however, been of great importance precisely because it has demonstrated that Christians can use the mass media for their own purposes, that an audience for this ministry exists, and that it is possible to present an alternative view to the dominant secular one. The coming of cable television will undoubtedly lead to a more depraved kind of entertainment than has thus far been seen on television. However, it also carries with it remarkable possibilities for the spread of religious values to a mass audience.

SEVEN

The Law and the Constitution

A S NOTED, America has, from the beginning, had a somewhat ambivalent attitude towards religion in public life. This stemmed from the fact that some of the Founding Fathers were essentially Deists, in the eighteenth-century sense, and some were believing Christians. Both streams helped to shape the American political system. It is possible to find precedent for both a rigid and a more permissive understanding of the principle of separation of church and state. Thomas Jefferson's personal suspicion of formal religion did not altogether prevail. Many customs grew up which demonstrate the esteem placed on religious faith: meetings of Congress are opened with a prayer and congressional chaplains appointed; the government commissions clergymen to serve as chaplains in the armed forces; the motto "In God We Trust" adorns official currency. Though the public schools eventually came to be the chief battleground between believers and secularizers, until at least World War II and longer in some places, the public schools frequently had a strongly religious character. Clergymen often served as teachers. The Bible was read. Prayers were recited every day. When the first Catholic schools were established in the mid-nineteenth century, it was not because the public schools were secular but because they were too Protestant.

Prior to World War II, there were few cases involving serious issues of religious freedom or separation of church and state that came before the Supreme Court. A loose, but comfortable, working relationship between religion and the public order was accepted by almost everybody. Perhaps the two major exceptions were an 1878 case (*Reynolds v. United States*) in which Utah Mormons were forbidden to practice polygamy and a 1925 case (*Pierce v. Society of Sisters*) in which the Court ruled that children could not be forced to attend public schools if suitable parochial schools were available.

At the opening of World War II, there were a spate of major court cases involving the right of conscientious objection to military service and the right not to salute the American flag if this violated an individual's religious convictions. The Jehovah's Witnesses were involved in these cases, and the Court essentially upheld their rights.

Beginning in 1947, however, and continuing unabated until the present, there have been an enormous number of court cases involving questions of religious freedom and separation of church and state. The number of such cases during these thirty-five years has far outstripped the number brought to court in the previous more than 150 years of the country's history. They have also raised all kinds of new issues, and the end result can justly be said to be a kind of revolution in the relationship between religion and American life.

Between 1948 and 1963, in a series of decisions, the Supreme Court essentially ruled that no religious exercise of any kind— readings from the Bible, general and non-denominational prayers—can be permitted in the public schools. Between 1947 and 1977, the Court banned most forms of public aid to religiously affiliated private schools, although it made a major exception in the case of colleges and universities. In effect, the Court established that public education must be secular. There was little disposition to permit government aid for private education for the children of those citizens who find this secularism unacceptable.

Many people have protested these decisions and decried their long-range impact on the country. The standard reply is always that, whatever hardships or seeming inequities they may impose on religious believers, such decrees are necessary in order to uphold the clear meaning of the First Amendment. To this is usually added the claim that religious believers should welcome such decrees, because their own religious freedom depends on the continued maintenance of strict separation of church and state.

The most obvious refutation of this claim has been noted. Throughout most of American history, arrangements existed which were not deemed violation of the Constitution. There has been a genuine revolution in judicial thinking since World War II. Furthermore, where public aid to religious schools is concerned, a number of countries comparable to the United States—Canada, Australia, the Netherlands—provide this aid equally to all religious schools, without suffering any unhappy political results.

If courts prior to 1947 did not generally think in these terms, what brought the revolution about? The simplest and best answer is that pressure groups organized themselves after the war precisely to bring it about. They had a vision of a secularized America, and they planned and executed a judicial and legal strategy to have that vision enshrined in law.

The three principal groups were the American Civil Liberties Union, probably the most important force for legal secularization and largely made up of people with a dogmatic belief in it; the American Jewish Congress, principally motivated by the estimation that Jews fare better in a secular than in a religious society; and Protestants and Other Americans United for Separation of Church and State, a group which at first simply opposed government aid to Catholic schools, but later changed its name to Americans United for Separation of Church and State and joined in the general secularist pressure.[1] These three groups, as well as others, raised issues the courts had never before considered and challenged practices which had always been tolerated. As important as the specific rulings they obtained was the fact that for the entire post-war era they have kept religion on the defensive in the American legal system through relentless pressure for secularization. Religious believers, rather than seeking to extend their influence in American society, have been reduced to protecting what seems like a steadily diminishing area in which they are allowed to have any influence at all.

Secularizers insist that the meaning of the First Amendment is plain and the decisions they seek are virtually incontestable. However, the personal beliefs of both plaintiffs and judges in such cases play an important role in explaining why sometimes extreme separationist attitudes have been accepted by the courts.

Probably the most successful lawyer arguing church-state separation cases since World War II has been Leo Pfeffer of the American Jewish Congress. Rather than a disinterested devotion to the Constitution, Pfeffer has confessed that he has a strong dislike of parochial schools. He argues plausibly that court decisions have brought about a "triumph of Secular Humanism."[2] In one case brought by the American Civil Liberties Union, the plaintiff was a woman who believed that religious education deforms children's minds.

William O. Douglas was one of the most influential Supreme Court justices in American history. From just before World War II until the late 1970s, he played a key role in a number of cases. Douglas was a thorough Secular Humanist who had little use for organized religion.[3] Equally influential with Douglas during the same period was Justice Hugo Black, who thought only "hypocrites" attend church and that good men do not need to attend.[4]

Modern Supreme Court decisions strongly reflect the assumptions of eighteenth-century rationalists, especially in their suspicion of religion as a divisive force in public life. (For example, the phrase "wall of separation of church and state," now treated as part of the Constitution itself, was a private metaphor of Thomas Jefferson and received almost no recognition by the Supreme Court until 1947.) Often they have referred to religious bodies as "sects," a word tending to imply narrowness and fanaticism. Justice Black, in a 1952 case (*Zorach v. Clauson*), stated explicitly that the Founding Fathers wanted

William O. Douglas (1898-1980) was one of the most influential Supreme Court justices in American history and perhaps the best example of the way in which judges have reinterpreted the Constitution to fit their personal biases. Although on one occasion he stated that the American political system presupposes a Supreme Being, on the whole Douglas' decisions tended to exclude religion from any meaningful role in public life and showed an almost obsessive fear that religion would damage the American state. On one occasion he wrote, "Every student of the subject ultimately faces the disorder which the mixture of sectarian and secular authority generates—either disorder between the church and the government, sometimes leading to the latter's overthrow by the former. It is discord between the sects with which we Americans have been most frequently concerned."

to guard against a situation in which religious believers "would sometimes torture, maim, and kill those they branded 'heretics,' 'atheists,' or 'agnostics.' " In a 1971 case (*Lemon v. Kurtzman*), Chief Justice Warren E. Burger wrote that, while political disagreement was generally a good thing, political division along religious lines is an evil which the courts must protect against.

Such opinions represent not careful judicial thought but the prejudices of the judges. These prejudices have now been enshrined in court decisions. (Not all the judges or lawyers who subscribe to such opinions are necessarily secularists themselves. Many religious believers have naively allowed themselves to be persuaded to accept the modern judicial revolution as expressing the true meaning of the Constitution.) Religion, guaranteed its liberty by the same First Amendment which forbids union of church and state, is now treated in law as a stepchild. Liberals who glory in the clash of "pluralistic" opinions in the political realm and who continuously seek to expand the scope of freedom of expression simultaneously want to restrict religious freedom as narrowly as possible. Such a desire, which can scarcely be defended logically, appears to stem from a belief that religion is of its nature a dangerous and destructive force. It is a feeling held by people who are personally comfortable only in a society where they sense that religion has no influence.

There have been blatant attempts to restrict religious freedom in the name of church-state separation. For example, in the mid-1970s Congress began forbidding the use of tax money to finance abortions. Suit was brought to undo that prohibition (*McRae v. Califano*, later *McRae v. Harris*) on the grounds that it reflected the concerns of religious believers, especially Catholics who were "imposing" their religious beliefs on others. Testimony in the case involved prying into the private lives of congressmen to determine their religious practices. The Supreme Court rejected the claim, but only by a 5-4 vote. Had one man voted differently, religious believers would, in effect, have been prohibited from politics, and only those people motivated by purely secular concerns would be allowed to influence public policy.

In a 1981 case (*Chess v. Widmar*), the Court ruled that a state university could not prohibit a student Bible-study group from meeting on campus if it granted meeting space to other groups. A university which granted meeting facilities to Marxists, homosexuals, and all kinds of other student organizations spent thousands of tax dollars to defend an attempt to suppress religious liberty. In another case (*Dittman v. Western Washington University,* 1980), presumably overturned by the Supreme Court's *Chess* ruling, a court held that a state university could impose restrictions on student religious groups which it did not impose on other groups, because religious groups pose "a clear and present danger" to separation of church and state.

Such cases result directly from what can be called the momentum of judicial secularism. As a result of thirty-five years of such cases, courts tend now to rule automatically against religious organizations and practices. Fanatic secularizers are encouraged to bring more and more outrageous cases. Not only do they show themselves at best indifferent to matters of religious liberty, their aim is obviously to restrict religion to private practice only. Every vestige of religious influence is to be expunged from public life, and religious believers are to be allowed a public voice only to the degree that they accept the secularist consensus. Even the private practice of religion is not completely secure. Some secularizers admit their desire to tax church property, which would probably have the effect of forcing many churches out of existence.

Largely in response to the enforced secularization of public schools, many Evangelical Protestants began establishing their own schools in the 1970s. This followed an example set earlier by Catholics, Lutherans, Christian Reformed, and some Jews. Such schools have been subject to a great deal of harassment from state agencies, in terms of academic accreditation, building codes, etc. The Federal government has tried to deny such schools tax exemption on the grounds that they are racially segregated. Only determined political action and expensive court cases have prevented many of these schools from being stifled at birth by hostile government officials.

While the courts have been extremely vigilant against the least signs of religious "entanglement" in politics, they have largely ignored the possibility that certain of their decisions may be giving unfair advantage to secularist groups. (One of the plaintiffs in the earliest post-war separationist case, *McCollum v. Board of Education,* later became president of the American Humanist Association and a signer of *Humanist Manifesto II.*)

Most people think of religion as belief in a personal God and, usually, membership in a church. For separationist purposes the courts think in the same way. Their strictures against "entanglement" generally apply only to organized religion in the traditional sense. However, where religious liberty is concerned, they have extended their definition as broadly as possible. In a decision concerning conscientious objection from military service (*Torcaso v. Watkins,* 1964), the Supreme Court explicitly listed Secular Humanism as a religion qualifying young men for such exemption. In a similar case (*United States v. Seeger,* 1965), the Court held that religion merely requires some belief that is the "equivalent" of belief in a Supreme Being, which could include almost anything.

This being the case, religious believers are entitled to wonder whether Secular Humanism, or some other non-theistic "religion," is now being given a privileged place in American society. Such a claim, so far, the courts have refused even to consider seriously. Far from being neutral, the American government is now in the position of favoring unbelief over belief and irreligion over religion, although the First Amendment merely requires that the government favor no particular church over other churches.

The issue becomes particularly explosive in the public schools. Many Christian parents believe their children are being exposed to Secular Humanist ideas under the guise of neutrality. By now practically all public schools have compulsory sex-education classes, taught in a variety of ways. Some parents object to these in principle, believing that sex education is a parental responsibility. Other parents would support such classes, but only if they included strong moral guidance as well as mere information. However, the moral principles of neither group are currently respected, except in cases where parents are able to bring pressure to bear on school officials. Thus students are often exposed to instruction which is morally repugnant to the parents and which tends to undermine parental teaching and authority. In the *McCollum* case the Supreme Court ruled against religious instruction on public-school property during school hours, even though children were not required to attend such classes, in part so that the children who did not attend might not be subject to embarrassment and harassment. However, the courts have shown no disposition to make a similar ruling in favor of children and parents with regard to sex-education classes. The long-range effect of court decisions has been to protect nonbelievers from religious influence in the public schools, while denying believers' rights to be protected from irreligious influences.

Some of the sex education in public schools undermines religious belief about sexuality in a passive way. It treats sex merely as a technical function and imparts information without any moral guidance as to its use. Increasingly, however, sex education is explicitly anti-religious. The leading "experts" in the field (such men as Lester Kirkendall and Sol Gordon, signers of *Humanist Manifesto II*) state bluntly that their purpose is to help students "get over their hangups." These are precisely the moral principles they learn from their parents or their church. The aim of sex education is often now to help young people to become "sexually active" in any way they choose, without moral scruple. This guilt-free hedonism is deemed necessary to a psychologically healthy existence. Parents who object strongly to such programs are nonetheless required to support them with their taxes and to allow their children to be part of them. This is a blatant violation of the rights of conscience that courts choose not to notice.

Sex education manifests the double standard which now affects public policy. In many schools representatives of

Planned Parenthood or similar organizations are allowed to conduct programs. These organizations actively promote abortion, contraception, and, implicitly, extra-marital sex. Efforts to ban these groups from the schools have largely been unsuccessful, though spokesmen for religious groups which might counteract this propaganda are banned. Sometimes representatives even of non-religious organizations promoting chastity are excluded. (The plaintiffs in the *McRae* case, including groups like the American Civil Liberties Union, argued that the personal religious affiliations of Congressmen are relevant to their political activities. Yet the same people do not deem relevant the official Humanist connections of the people who plan and promote sex-education programs in the schools.)

While sex education is the most sensitive, it is not the only area where values collide in the public schools. Religiously conservative parents are often accused of being "book burners." Yet the law forbids the use of religious books in the classroom, and some schools even exclude them from the libraries. At the same time, schools may employ books with an anti-religious bias or which otherwise deeply affront parental values.

Increasingly controversial is the employment of the techniques of "values clarification" in the schools. Although ostensibly "neutral" with regard to values, this technique in fact undermines values children have learned from their parents or from the church. It is a system in which children are encouraged to regard all questions of belief as "open" matters of opinion. Students who appear to be firm in their beliefs are encouraged to call them into question. The ultimate end of such programs is to instill the idea that all values are relative, the result of mere personal choice.

When criticized, Humanists insist piously that they are committed to no particular position with regard to moral values. Their only desire is to see to it that all beliefs obtain a fair hearing. The myth of neutrality, accepted even by many Christians, is the most useful weapon secularists have in dominating public institutions. No policy decision, no matter how apparently innocuous, is devoid of assumptions about values. The determination of what courses should be in a school curriculum, how they should be taught, what textbooks should be used, how teachers should be trained and recruited, what kind of discipline should exist in the school, and a host of other things all give moral tone and direction to the school. There is no such thing as neutrality. Those who assert that there is are, consciously or unconsciously, using that idea to promote their own favored values.

Among other things, the courts have refused to recognize that banning all manifestations of religion from the public schools is itself a value judgment. Even if teachers are scrupulous in refraining from any even implicit anti-religious stance (not all are), the absence of religion from the school itself conveys a powerful message to students. The modern school has undertaken to instruct students in everything society deems important, from science and foreign languages to first aid and the skills of driving. If religion is absent, it is reasonable to assume, it is because society regards it either as unimportant or false. Throughout history, in all cultures of the world, religion has played a profoundly important part in the lives of people, permeating every aspect of existence. When public schools ignore religion they are doing violence to reality itself and giving their students an inadequate education.

The standard secularist reply is that students should learn religion at home or in church. That is begging the question. Schools are set up, and children required to attend them, precisely because it is believed that parents are incapable of giving them all the education they need; this is the standard argument for sex education. Many devout parents lack the ability to educate their children in religion in any systematic way. Sunday school or other church-sponsored religious education lasts only at best a few hours a week and cannot compete with five full days of religionless education. Americans increasingly grow up religiously illiterate, often possessing inchoate religious feelings which they have difficulty expressing or understanding.

When various groups go to court to fight even the blandest and most innocuous prayers in the public schools, or to protest nativity scenes set up in public at Christmas time, they affirm the importance of those symbols. In effect, they argue that such symbols are powerful and have a negative affect on non-believers. But these same secularizers also argue that such symbols are mere tokens which do no good, hence that religious believers should acquiesce in their banishment. Negative symbolism is as powerful as positive. When young people in particular learn that it is forbidden to pray or read the Bible in school, to mention the name of God, or to sing Christmas carols, they cannot help but receive the impression that their society regards religion as something dangerous or unwholesome.

Many secularists are hypocritical on this issue. They proclaim a neutrality in which all groups have equal rights and none enjoys any privileges. In fact, they have created a situation in which their own godless viewpoint is established by law. Privately, many of them are quite aware of the negative affects these decisions have on religion. They consciously make use of public policy to damage religion, especially among the younger generation. Since the time of the Enlightenment there has always been an opinion in the West that deplores the authority which parents and churches have to form young minds. Now secularists manipulate the law to suppress that influence as much as possible.

Not all secularists are opposed to the authority of the family, but many are. It is inevitable that militant secularists will attack that authority, because it is the chief means by which religious belief is handed down. Just as there are humanistic psychologists who define religion as a sickness, so there are humanistic psychologists who define family life as essentially a pathology (for example, the Englishman David Cooper, in his book, *The Death of the Family*).

Just as court cases have steadily whittled away at the authority of organized religion, so they now whittle away at the authority of families. In *Planned Parenthood v. Danforth* (1976) the Supreme Court ruled that minor children may receive abortions without parental knowledge or consent. Public agencies now routinely distribute contraceptives to minors without parental knowledge, a process in which the schools often cooperate. The rationale for this is that adolescents are now "sexually active" anyway, and it is necessary that they be protected against pregnancy. But those who use this argument never ask whether sex-education programs are not themselves a major cause of this sexual "activeness." Furthermore, while such activity is referred to as though it were a regrettable fact of life, some people in sensitive positions actually regard it as a positive good. They want to exclude parents from the process precisely because they fear parents would be a restraining force on their children's behavior.

Although it is presently imprudent to say so publicly, many secularists regard it as equally regrettable that parents have the opportunity to inculcate religious beliefs in their children from an early age. The determined secularization of the public schools and the active discouragement of private religious schools aim to minimize that influence as much as possible. Some secularists eagerly look forward to the day when a universal system of government sponsored day-care centers will take responsibility for children's upbringing soon after they leave the cradle.

To date, there have been few legal challenges to parental authority in matters of religion. However, in a case involving the refusal of Amish parents to send their children to public schools (*Wisconsin v. Yoder*, 1972), Justice Douglas wondered whether parents have the right to "impose" their own religious beliefs on their children. The Court ruled in favor of the Amish, but there is little doubt that Douglas's speculations represent the thinking of at least some secularists.

To date, there have also been only a few tentative attacks by secularists on the authority which churches have over their members. One reason for fearing the proposed Equal Rights Amendment to the Constitution, however, is that if it were enacted some women would undoubtedly go to court to demand their "right" to become clergy in denominations which do not

Harry Blackmun is the Supreme Court justice who wrote the decision in 1973 which established a woman's "right" to have an abortion, a decision which another justice aptly characterized as "an exercise in raw judicial power." The decision has been widely criticized even by those who are not opposed to abortion. It typifies the way in which courts have cavalierly overturned deeply ingrained moral beliefs and substituted a kind of dogmatic moral relativism. In his decision Blackmun took note of religious and philosophical arguments about the humanity of the unborn child, but only to dismiss them.

permit this. Although in general the courts have refrained from intruding into the internal affairs of religious groups, there is no guarantee that future courts would not reverse that practice. Where homosexual-rights laws have been passed in some cities, attempts have been made to force religious schools to hire homosexual teachers. Court rulings on this question, because confined to the local level, have been inconsistent.

The secularists' political and judicial onslaught since 1947 would not have been possible except for the inattention and passivity of religious believers. As each new case has been handed down, there have been cries of anguish and outrage but little more. Aside from a few unsuccessful attempts to pass legislation to reverse court decisions, religious believers remained politically uninvolved. Many of them were and are largely oblivious to what was and is happening around them.

The Supreme Court's decision recognizing abortion as a woman's consitutional "right" (*Roe v. Wade,* 1973, written by Harry Blackmun) probably woke the sleeping religious giant. The various anti-abortion movements have been far more successful than anyone could have predicted in 1973. In addition, concern for the abortion issue has directly stimulated political action on a host of other questions. The systematic pattern of denial of religious values in public life is now becoming apparent even to previously complacent people.

Most Christians probably find combative political action distasteful. It is also true that the kingdom of God is not achieved by political means. Nonetheless, political activity on behalf of religious values is essential merely to protect those values from being trampled and to insure the continuation of religious liberty. The cries of outrage directed at Christian political-action groups once again indicate that such groups are effective. For the first time in years, secularists are beginning to feel that not everything is going as they would like.

EIGHT

The Secularization of the Churches

IF THE PRIMARY conflict in America were merely between church members and non-church members there would be little reason to worry about secularism. Church members still constitute a clear majority and organized groups of secularists are relatively few and small.

As noted, secularists have influence out of proportion to their numbers, because they are situated in strategic places in society. However, even these positions would not be translated into the systematic secularization of American life if the numerical size of organized religion were an accurate measure of its influence. The unfortunate fact is that organized religion on the whole is a rather feeble bulwark against secularization. Either the churches do not fully comprehend the problem and do not strongly oppose it, or, in some cases, the churches themselves are deeply affected by it. Ironically, to a degree the churches themselves are primary vehicles by which secularism is spread.

During the Enlightenment, the clergy were not particularly effective in countering anti-religious ideas. Some clergy even became partisans of the Enlightenment. Many of those who did not embrace it openly nonetheless showed themselves tolerant of ideas which were undermining faith. The Enlightenment began a process which has carried through Western religion to the present day. In this process, some leading religious thinkers have concentrated their energies on reconciling faith and

115

modern culture, primarily the culture of skeptical intellectuals. This has meant that, more often than not, orthodox believers find themselves not only in tension with secular culture but, more seriously, in tension with compromising members of their own faith. (Primarily this is true of Christianity, the dominant religion of the West. However, it has also led to a tripartite division of Judaism into Orthodox, Conservative, and Reform.)

At the beginning of the nineteenth century, the German Protestant theologian Friederich Schleiermacher addressed himself to Christianity's "cultured despisers." Schleiermacher's aim was to overcome their contempt and make secular intellectuals take religion seriously. In the process, he set in motion a chain of religious thinking which has now become dominant in a good part of modern Christianity.

In principle, the effort to reach Christianity's "cultured despisers" should be praised. If nothing else, it is one of the obligations of evangelization, however unpromising it may seem. It is also important to the future of Christianity. A religion which totally abdicated the intellectual realm would soon lose almost all social influence and be confined to rather isolated pockets of uneducated people.

The problem lies in how the effort to persuade the skeptic is made. Schleiermacher's method, generally followed by religious modernizers ever since, had two possibly fatal flaws. It approached the skeptic, as it were, hat in hand, placing Christianity in a deferential and self-deprecating posture. It also took prevailing ideas in the secular intellectual world as normative, to which Christianity was expected to conform. In effect Schleiermacher and his numerous religious descendants said, "We will save as much of our faith as can be reconciled with secular thought. Having thus purified it, we hope that you secularists will agree to respect us."

The word "liberal" came into use just after the French Revolution, at the time Schleiermacher was writing. Soon it was common to speak of "liberal Christianity." Few words in the language are more slippery than "liberal." It originally merely meant someone who is generous, especially with money. After

1800, it came to mean someone who had a commitment to the expansion of freedom. Generally, liberals were admirers of the French Revolution, while admitting its excesses. Liberals of the early nineteenth century strove to be consistent. They saw freedom as something which should be expanded across the board. Thus they favored freedom of speech, of the press, of assembly, of religion, and free elections. (There were inconsistencies. Sometimes they curtailed freedom of religion when they regarded the church as the enemy of progress.) In economic matters, nineteenth-century liberals tended to be close to what are now called conservatives. They favored economic freedom, which for them meant the right of businessmen to do business free of government control.

It was generally the case in the nineteenth century that orthodox religious believers were political conservatives. They feared the long-term affects of the godless French Revolution and liberal governments were often hostile to religion. However, this connection between theological orthodoxy and political conservatism was mainly a historical accident. There were many exceptions to it.

More basic, perhaps, was the connection between political and religious liberalism. To a great extent, religious liberals transferred the ideas of political liberalism into the religious realm. On the practical level this meant that they were often naive about the implications of certain government policies. Religious liberals permitted, and often actively promoted, the secularization of Western education, for example. They also acquiesced in the idea that church-state separation should logically mean the complete secularization of politics. They underestimated the degree of hostility to religion of some liberal governments, and they opposed organized political action by religious groups.

Religious liberals applied the principle of "freedom" to matters of religion in roughly the same way it was applied to politics. To a certain extent this meant that they favored the democratization of the churches. More seriously, they applied it to belief itself. They became resistant or actively hostile to authority in religion. They exalted individual human judgment to the point where it sometimes did not seem to matter whether the individual came to know truth, but merely whether free personal inquiry was exercised. Religious liberals tended to develop a spirit of resistance or hostility towards the very idea of religious orthodoxy and religious authority.

This attitude, coupled with the habit of deferring to secular intellectuals, meant that in practice religious liberals frequently came to doubt, deny, or at least hold in suspension certain well established teachings of Christianity. In any apparent conflict between the teachings of religion and the theories of secular intellectuals, they tended automatically to the side of the latter. This did not always mean outright rejection of traditional Christian teaching. That would have meant leaving the church altogether, and most liberals wanted to play the role of mediator between the secular culture and the church. It did mean that they did not strongly affirm Christian doctrines or that they continually reformulated those doctrines in such a way that their meaning was, at best, ambiguous.

During the first half of the nineteenth century, religious liberalism primarily focussed on controversies over the Scripture, especially controversies provoked by scientific findings. Debate raged over the age of the world, the way in which it had been created, and other matters relevant to the physical sciences. This in turn called into question the authority of Scripture itself. How literally could it be read? How much historical truth did it contain? Such controversies raged not only between religious believers and skeptical scientists but also within the churches themselves. Liberals often lost particular battles. Some liberal professors were dismissed from seminary faculties, for example. But, in the long run, in many denominations, they won the war. (The establishment of Protestant seminaries in America was a reflection of the fact that orthodox Protestants were losing influence at the colleges—Harvard, Yale, Princeton—which they had founded in colonial times. Before too many generations, however, newer seminaries were being founded because of dissatisfaction with existing ones.)

Towards the end of the century, the area of conflict broadened and became even more crucial to the credibility of orthodox faith. In brief, this conflict can be said to have been over the nature of historical consciousness. To what extent are ideas and beliefs the product of the historical periods in which they are conceived, and to what extent is it possible to believe in eternal truths which transcend historical limitations? The controversy over the Book of Genesis turned out to be a preliminary skirmish in this great battle. Earlier liberals had wanted to modify the way in which Christians read the first book of the Bible. Later liberals wanted to extend the same modifications to the entire Bible and to all other Christian documents.

Gradually, liberals at the turn of the twentieth century came to believe that all religious formulations—Scripture, creeds, confessional statements, moral principles—were the products of a developing human consciousness which changed through history. In 1900, most liberals still believed in some direct and special divine inspiration, but they did not believe that this worked to guarantee the truth of every authoritative Christian pronouncement. Instead they saw religious believers struggling, as part of the common human condition, towards some grasp of truth. Aided by divine grace, they arrived periodically at expressions of truth which seemed final and authoritative. Each time they discovered that these were inadequate and began the process again.

Most liberals at the turn of the century still believed that the central teachings of Christianity were virtually beyond question. But they often interpreted these in new ways, and there were other church teachings which were not regarded as sacrosanct. Since personal inquiry was the principal means by which religious truth is discovered, although guided by divine inspiration, private judgment was not infallible. Thus few of the official teachings could be regarded as infallible either.

No theologian in the history of the church would have hesitated to admit that all doctrinal formulations fall short of encompassing the infinity of divine truth. There is always the possibility of new doctrinal formulations. What was radically new about the liberalism of the late nineteenth century was that not only were past formulations regarded as incomplete, they could also be regarded as false. Old formulas were discarded not in order to express more profoundly what they contained but to be rid of them entirely.

Most liberals in 1900 were still committed Christians. They thought of their work as that of making Christianity more credible to skeptics and of protecting it from attack by removing the objects of those attacks. Gradually liberals devised what might be called a concentric-circles strategy. Briefly, it amounted to a series of decisions to abandon, one after another, certain dimensions of Christian teaching which were regarded as no longer credible, for the purpose of protecting other more central dimensions. Liberals, in effect, decided to save Christianity through a series of strategic retreats, until they reached what they thought would be high and unassailable ground.

Their key argument was that divine revelation had become crusted over, throughout history, with many things not essential to it. In earlier times these "encrustations" had helped make Christianity more credible and understandable. Now they did the opposite. These historical accretions had to be stripped away so that the basic Christian message could shine forth unencumbered. To a degree, this strategy is a necessary one, which all Christians must follow. Every age has its own forms of infidelity, and every age is capable of misunderstanding the gospel in different ways. Thus it is necessary, in each age, to inquire as to misunderstandings which may have come down from the past.

The fatal flaw in the liberal strategy, however, was the lack of any firm conviction as to the nature of divine truth. Liberals at the turn of the century believed ardently that God had inspired the Bible and, if they were Catholics, the church. But they were unprepared to say how and to what extent. They took it for granted that certain Christian beliefs were beyond question, but they had no principles for determining which ones, or why.

Thus the history of modern religious liberalism is the history of the gradual abandonment of one circular wall after another. The result has not been, as the defenders had hoped, to make the remaining walls the more secure. It has simply rendered them all the more vulnerable. Each generation of liberals ends by conceding the wall which the previous generation had thought impregnable.

This can perhaps best be seen by tracing a few typical progressions in liberal religious thinking, beginning with the earliest positions and moving to the present:

> While the Bible as a whole is inspired, certain passages not compatible with modern science, e.g., the creation accounts, are human inventions.

> While certain miracles central to the Christian faith, especially Christ's resurrection from the dead, must be believed, other miracle accounts in the Scripture are merely expressions of simple people.

> Christians must believe that Christ rose from the dead. However, they need not believe that the tomb was empty on Easter morning. The Resurrection can be understood as his continuing spiritual presence among his disciples.

> While Jesus was certainly the only begotten Son of God, secondary beliefs merely meant to reinforce that, e.g., his virgin birth, need not be believed.

> While God was certainly present in Jesus in a special way, it is not meaningful to speak of him as the Son of God in the traditional sense.

> What is central to Christianity is the message of salvation brought by Christ and uniquely achieved through him. The circumstances of this redemption are subject to varying interpretations.

> To speak of man's being "saved" by Jesus presents problems since many people do not feel a need of being saved. Jesus is better seen as the greatest moral teacher in the history of the world and Christianity as the pinnacle of world religions.

> To regard Jesus as unique, and his teaching as superior to

that of other religious leaders like the Buddha, is arrogant cultural chauvinism. God reveals himself in every culture in different ways.

Whatever one may think about the various religions of the world, what is crucial is to believe in an all-powerful God who created the universe and sustains it in being.

The word "God" is one which men have used throughout history to refer to some ultimate reality which is the deepest dimension of existence. Personalization of God, and talk about his being creator and lord of the universe, are merely means men have used to make that awareness more vivid to themselves.

In effect, the liberal strategy, far from enabling the core of Christian belief to stand out more brightly as accretions are stripped away, has made the whole of Christianity merely a series of accretions, fated to be given up one by one. Having abandoned any belief in ultimate religious authority in favor of a belief primarily in the efficacy of personal searching, liberals have no basis for remaining faithful to even the most fundamental Christian doctrines.

The ostensible purpose of the liberal strategy is, as noted, to make Christianity more credible to the skeptic and to render it less vulnerable to attack. Here too the strategy has often achieved the opposite of what was intended. There is practically no example in modern times of a prominent nonbeliever being persuaded of the credibility of Christianity because of liberal attempts at persuasion, or who has embraced liberal Christianity as a credible alternative to orthodoxy. Those nonbelieving intellectuals who have become converts—like Jacques Maritain, T.S. Eliot, and C.S. Lewis—have almost all been attracted to orthodox Christianity, and have spent their lives defending and elaborating that orthodoxy.

The reasons for this are not hard to see. The skeptic who pays close attention to the religious liberals (most do not) may agree with what the liberal is doing and may applaud his effort. But he is not persuaded to respect religion, because he finds in the liberal strategy merely confirmation of his own assumption that Christianity is false and outmoded. Sooner or later, he reasons, liberal Christians will come to the same conclusion. Meanwhile they must go through the agony of redefining their beliefs in such a way as to lessen the trauma of their abandonment of faith. Liberalism in religion has never been a way into faith; it has always been a way out.

Liberals also overlook something else crucial to religion. So great is their concentration on making their beliefs credible to skeptics that they tend to think of religion primarily as intellectual. True religion, however, cuts to the very roots of a person's being. Religion properly understood is supposed to transform men's lives totally. Converts have always been attracted by a religion which promises that. If they come to realize their need for salvation, they will feel little attraction to a religion which seems unsure as to what salvation means, or how it is achieved. A loosely defined religion, subject to endless revisions in keeping with the preferences of individuals, has little appeal to those outside the faith. It serves mainly those who chafe against their inherited faith and are looking for ways to make it less demanding.

The cultural mood of the late nineteenth century tended to promote religious liberalism. This was due, on the intellectual level, largely to the strong attacks made on religion by skeptics and to developments in the secular sciences which seemed to call for rethinking of traditional beliefs. Similar forces were at work on the popular level. The late nineteenth century was an age of great optimism, brought on mainly by the visible signs of material progress generated by technological and industrial development. It seemed as though man, given enough time, could do anything. There was an almost mandatory belief in "Progress," understood largely in material terms.

This made some people atheists, others agnostics. On the whole, however, Victorian respectability demanded religion, which was thought of as undergirding the whole moral system. For many people the idea of progress in worldly matters automatically transferred to matters of religion. (Queen Victoria herself, stereotyped as rigid and old-fashioned, was something of a religious liberal.)

Since the spirit of the age was optimistic, it demanded an optimistic faith, which liberalism was prepared to provide. In particular, religious liberalism de-emphasized human sinfulness and the corresponding need of redemption. It was also skeptical about miracles and divine intervention in human affairs. These seemed to go against the scientific spirit and man's sense of self-reliance and emancipation.

One form of liberalism reduced Christianity to a system of ethics. Christ was primarily a great ethical teacher. All the "irrelevant" doctrines of the church were quietly discarded. This did not solve the fundamental problem. What was the basis of Christian ethics? If they had any authoritative basis, it had to be Scripture. Yet one could not take the Scripture authoritatively in its moral teachings and ignore the rest of it.

Some liberals hit upon a strategy of saying that Christian moral teachings (as in the Sermon on the Mount) are the highest and most profound expressions ever made of natural human morality. This morality is rooted in man's very nature and not dependent on religious authority. The moral Babel of the later twentieth century has cast into severe doubt the idea that there even is such an ethics. It has also been a strategy which leads to the progressive emptying of Christian morality of all content. Liberals simply stick the Christian label on any moral position they happen to find persuasive at a given time.

Prior to the nineteenth century, virtually all Protestantism was Evangelical in the sense of being committed to the basic authority of the Bible. Evangelicalism, sometimes later called Fundamentalism, emerged as a self-conscious movement within the church shortly after the turn of the century precisely because of the growing realization of how deeply liberalism had seeped into the churches. Major battles were fought in most denominations, which often led to schisms, new seminaries, and new attempts to define the essence of the Christian faith. In the Catholic Church, an incipient theological liberalism was condemned by Pope Pius X in 1907 under the name of Modernism.

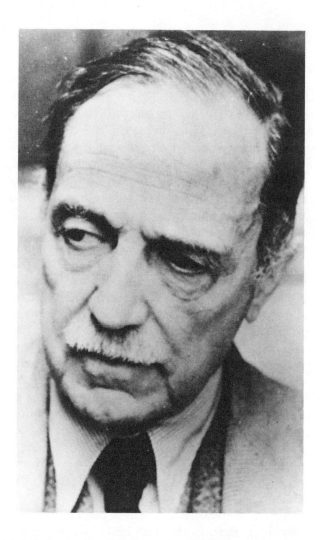

Rudolph Bultmann has dominated liberal Scripture scholarship in the past fifty years through his attempts to "demythologize" the Bible, that is, to strip away all those aspects of it which he regards as no longer relevant to the modern age. Although Bultmann believes in God and in the continued relevance of the biblical message, in practice his approach tends to make Christian belief captive to contemporary cultural and intellectual prejudices. Thus Bultmann proposes as an argument: "Or let us simply think of the newspapers. Have you read anywhere in them that political or social or economic events are performed by supernatural powers such as God, angels, or demons?"

World War I dealt a serious blow to liberalism, in that it destroyed much of the optimism and uncritical faith in progress on which liberalism had fed. Karl Barth, whose first book appeared during the war, led the way for Protestants to return to a more biblically based faith. What the war did was to shatter easy complacencies about progress and the inevitable good fruits of human action. It restored a strong sense of sin and of man's very feeble control over his own destiny. It once again made redemption central, and restored the sense of being under divine judgment. The political disorders of the 1920s in Europe, the Great Depression and the rise of totalitarianism during the 1930s, and World War II all reinforced this. Although religious liberalism by no means died, it went into a long eclipse.

Gradually the prosperity of the post-war world brought about its revival. It was slow, because the mood for a decade and more following the war was rather orthodox in most respects. Victory over the Axis powers had given a new appreciation for traditions and beliefs.

Liberalism had its second great flowering during the 1960s. The work of Harvey Cox was its most influential American expression. Internationally, its chief spokesman was probably the German theologian Rudolf Bultmann, with his radical attempts to "demythologize" Scripture. In the Catholic Church, the Second Vatican Council of 1962-65 was the occasion for restless Catholics to emulate liberal Protestants. A concerted effort was made to interpret the Council as ratifying that liberalism.

In this second flowering, liberalism was considerably more radical than in its first. In the mid-1960s, there was a flurry of controversy over the "death-of-God" theology. This was essentially an updating of Nietzsche's proclamation that God (or the idea of God) is dead. What was new and startling was that now this proclamation was made by professedly Christian theologians and was called a theology. This "death-of-God" theology was rather quickly dismissed, even by many liberals. But what these "theologians" had done was to lift the veil briefly to show what really lay behind religious liberalism. The veil will certainly be raised again at some future time, and will remain up.

In this second flowering, religious liberalism has, to a great extent, also abandoned any claim that it is attempting to save classical Christianity or to win over the skeptics. Many religious liberals no longer have enough interest in classical Christian teachings even to bother reformulating or denying them. They take for granted their irrelevance. Many of them also do not think the church worth saving in anything like its traditional form. Many liberals are now more or less frank emissaries from the secular culture to the church, seeking to win the church over to the secular agenda.

Many forces combined to bring about this situation, among them the fashionable Continental philosophy of Existentialism, which bloomed after World War II. The Existentialists (Jean-Paul Sartre and Albert Camus particularly) talked about the anguish of life and of man's sense of being thrown into an absurd and meaningless world. Man has total freedom because he must now make his own world. Although there have been Christians who have made use of Existentialist insights (for example, the Catholic philosopher Gabriel Marcel), in the end it seems impossible to reconcile Existentialism and Christianity. Sartre and Camus were both atheists. Belief in God eliminates the sense of meaninglessness which the Existentialists posit as central to human experience.

But modern religious liberals, in effect, argue that every human being is obligated to experience this meaninglessness. For practical purposes there is no difference between the believer and the nonbeliever. Both are thrown into a hostile universe. Both find themselves baffled by the mysteries of existence. Neither can claim any help except the stumbling, fragmented process of human trial and error.

Implicit in this position is the most fundamental error of contemporary religious liberalism—its denial of authentic divine revelation. Present-day liberals do not truly believe that God revealed himself to man or that man finds meaning in life through obedience to the divine plan. They believe that all

Jean-Paul Sartre (1905-80) was virtually the founder of the contemporary philosophy of Existentialism. Although it was reported that on his deathbed he expressed belief in God, most of his life was spent denying that possibility. The philosophy of Existentialism holds that man is thrown into an essentially meaningless universe and is thus radically free to create the kind of world he chooses. As with Freud, Nietzsche, and other modern thinkers, God for Sartre was merely an illusion: "To be man means to reach towards being God. Or if you prefer, man fundamentally is the desire to be God."

supposed manifestations of revelation (the Bible) are essentially human creations. Whereas earlier religious liberals still held the Bible as central to their beliefs, contemporary liberals, when frank, are likely to see it as only one source of guidance among many, and not necessarily the most important. They have no difficulty negating things in the Bible they find inconvenient.

Religious liberalism is not the same as secularism. However, it is the means by which secularism enters the churches. It is fair to say that the most advanced religious liberals now have an outlook on life not essentially different from secularists, and they want to convert the church to that same outlook. They are apostles of unbelief, endlessly telling believers that they should no longer accept this or that teaching of Christianity. Finally, they negate all of them.

The most basic tenets of contemporary religious liberalism could perhaps be stated as follows:

All religious beliefs are the product of developing human experience and inquiry and, as such, have no special authoritative status.

All moral principles are of the same nature. Hence there are no moral absolutes. Right and wrong are essentially determined in accordance with the needs and desires of individuals in particular situations.

Two thousand years of Christianity are largely irrelevant to the present, and those aspects of that history still revelant can be made so only by radical reinterpretation.

Christianity has no claim to superior status among the religions of the world. All the great religions partake of portions of the truth in accordance with their own cultures and historical situations.

The history of Christianity is filled with errors and pernicious evils perpetrated by the church. This is true not only of the unworthy behavior of individual Christians, or of the distortion of Christian teaching, but of the very nature of historical Christianity.

Since religion is mostly the result of human searching and

experience, men find their surest and most reliable guides not primarily in the church or in Christian doctrine but in secular intellectual disciplines and human experience generally. The teaching of the church must be endlessly reformulated in accordance with these.

The liberal habit of looking over the shoulder to see what the skeptics think has become a general surrender to secular authority. The church is kept in a perpetual state of judgment before the world, repeatedly apologizing for its past errors and promising to do better in the future.

This liberalism, now almost indistinguishable from secularism, manifests itself in a number of ways.

1. Authoritative Christian documents, whether the Bible, historic creeds, or other statements, are either ignored as irrelevant or employed only to the degree that they seem to fit with current secular preoccupations.

2. Worship is regarded primarily as a human experience, not as a way of paying homage to God. Worship services (and sermons) are structured in such a way as to create a sense of community and belonging among the worshippers, with little regard for the transcendental dimension of the action.

3. Christians are not encouraged to have a strong personal sense of their dependence on God's Providence. God is thought not to intervene in the affairs of men, so that human problems are to be solved through human means only.

4. A personal sense of fulfillment or satisfaction is taken as the ultimate criterion of truth. Thus religious doctrines and practices are kept or discarded to the degree that they seem "meaningful" to the individual. The concept of objective religious truth is effectively denied. The purpose of religion is thought to be the achievement of a subjective sense of spiritual well-being by the individual.

5. All morality is provisional only. Many of the past moral teachings of the church, especially with regard to sex, are now seen as pernicious and deforming. Since personal "need" is the ultimate guide to conduct and since personal fulfillment is the

chief aim of existence, the liberal Christian often leads a life at odds with traditional Christian morality.

Much of liberal religion is now empty, its content having been gradually drained over the years. This has created a tremendous spiritual vacuum. In many liberal churches it would be difficult to discover why people belong, or what they find there. (In fact membership in the liberal churches has been declining.) Such a vacuum cannot exist forever, and strenuous attempts have been made to fill it. Essentially, this has meant throwing the resources of the church wholeheartedly behind certain secular movements which seem to promise a better world.

There is a curious irony in liberal Christianity. As liberal spokesmen find it less and less possible to speak with authority on subjects Christianity has historically spoken about with authority, they find it easier and easier to speak dogmatically on subjects where the church has no special competence. Typically, a liberal clergyman will not know exactly what he thinks about Jesus, the Bible, or adultery, but does know exactly what he thinks about the politics of El Salvador or the Equal Rights Amendment, and he expresses himself forthrightly. Such dogmatism stems directly from the liberal's loss of a sense of the supernatural and of eternity. He has become a secularist in the literal sense of one who lives for this world only. Liberalism now assumes that the chief purpose of religion is to create a better world, because it is fairly certain that there is no world beyond this one. The model for a better world is taken over, more or less totally and without change, from various secular groups.

In particular, the idea of Christian compassion is used to support and justify any social group which claims to be oppressed and demands "justice." Although they probably often use the words as mere figures of speech, liberals profess to find the hand of the Spirit (now, perhaps, not the Holy Spirit but the Spirit of the Age) in every movement for "progress" and against "oppression"—Women's Liberation, Third World guerillas, "gay rights," etc. For most religious liberals, this is a rather mild commitment, although a firm one. They espouse social change just enough to give direction and substance to their religion, not enough to be fanatical. But other liberal Christians are quite fanatical.

Some look for the Kingdom of God on earth. They support Marxists and Marxist regimes, for example, because they have essentially accepted Karl Marx's dichotomy between belief in eternity and the achievement of a perfect society on earth. Despite the Marxist record of brutality and suppression of freedom, they support Marxist movements, because Marxists alone seem to have the commitment, the determination, even the ruthlessness to go beyond mere social reform to the total transformation of society. Certain modern Christians are so secularized that they in effect make "the Revolution" their god. (This attitude is found, to varying degrees, in the World Council of Churches.)

Orthodox Christians sometimes make the mistake of saying the church should stay out of politics. Since all human actions stand under divine judgment, there is no way in principle whereby certain of those actions can be declared to be "political" only. In principle, the church must take an interest in political questions with a view to their moral implications. What is objectionable about so many contemporary Christians is not their political involvement but their virtual deification of politics and their apparent failure to bring a truly Christian perspective to bear on political questions. Rather than missionaries from the church to the world, they are the reverse.

It is important that orthodox Christians also notice that secularism invaded the churches for what were essentially good motives. In almost every case, the root of religious secularization can be found in an idea which is authentically Christian— compassion for the oppressed, respect for human reason, acknowledgement of one's own failings. Good but naive Christians are sometimes confused by appeals to their better natures in ways which distort genuine Christianity subtly but seductively.

Since militant secularism has made sex the chief focal point of its attack on religion, sex has inevitably become a crucial point of conflict in the churches as well. There is no more revealing index of the secularism to which many Christians have succumbed than their acceptance, and in some cases their endorsement, of the sexual revolution in all its ramifications— abortion, divorce, extra-marital sex, homosexuality. In no area is there a clearer indication of the way some Christians use religious language to justify whatever the avant-garde of the secular culture advocates.

In a sense, liberal Christians now have no choice but to accept movements like the sexual revolution. They have exalted human experience as the ultimate criterion of truth, and they have convinced themselves that the Spirit is moving in history. Therefore, every seemingly important historical movement must be invested with religious significance. Since the late nineteenth century, liberal Christians have been optimists about human nature and therefore, to a great extent, optimists about human society as well. They are not comfortable opposing trends in society which seem to be those of the future.

Because of its exaltation of personal experience as the ultimate criterion of truth, liberal Christianity cannot have a very strong sense of sin. It has in large measure adopted the principles of Humanistic Psychology as a way of avoiding sin. But the abolition of sin is not merely a matter of ignoring it. The problem of guilt remains. Increasingly, those who absolutize their own experiences in the religious and moral realm are driven to greater and greater defiance of established moral and religious absolutes. They need to deny more and more of their religious heritage in order to feel entirely secure in their liberation. So liberal Christians are often found, along with militant secularists, not only justifying behavior which Christianity has traditionally held to be sinful, but denouncing the church, often in bitter and abusive terms, for its refusal to condone such sins.

Although liberal Christians usually deny they are secularists, Secular Humanists recognize kindred souls. The *Humanist Manifesto I,* for example, included phrases like, "Certainly religious institutions, their ritualistic forms, ecclesiastical methods, and communal activities must be reconstituted as rapidly as experience allows, in order to function effectively in the modern world,"[1] a belief which could be easily expressed by liberal Christians. The leading Humanist Paul Kurtz applauds the "humanization and liberalization" of Catholicism.[2] In general, Humanists tend to support dissident Christians like the Catholic theologian Hans Küng, whom they see as conceding most of the criticisms Humanists have made of religion.

Secularism in the churches does not simply mean a kind of worldly-mindedness, absence of religious fervor, or a tendency to ignore religious principles most of the time. Such easy worldliness has always existed. Preachers have warned against it for centuries. Secularism requires a certain amount of self-consciousness and deliberate decision. It implies a recognition of the difference between Christian and secular values and a choice of the latter. It implies also an actual hostility to Christianity, and the conviction that religious belief has pernicious effects on people.

Strange though it may seem, there is a good deal of Secular Humanism, in this sense, among professed Christians. Even among active church members. Even among the clergy. Liberal Christianity now inexorably gives rise to attitudes which are basically secularist in nature. Some Christians devote most of their energies not to converting nonbelievers but to attacking alleged deformities within the churches themselves. Often these "deformities" are the heart of the Christian message.

Many church members have no idea to what extent the message they receive from their religious leaders, often in Sunday sermons, reflects not authentic Christianity but secularism disguised in religious garb. Frequently the preacher himself does not realize what he is saying. He merely repeats what he has been taught in the seminary or has read in the religious press. This rather bizarre situation has come about in part because of the general religious illiteracy of American society. Many people have a vague sense that what they are hearing is not quite orthodox, but they have no ability to say why, nor to make a rigorous analysis of it.

Hans Küng, the most widely read contemporary Catholic theologian, exemplifies the way in which secular values are spread even within the churches in the name of "renewal." While Küng affirms the existence of God and the essential truth of Christianity, in practice he tends to rob most traditional Christian teachings of their power and authority. He proposes instead a highly secular understanding of what it means to be a Christian: "Reconciliation and everyday service to our fellow man have priority over service to God."

Thus, by a strange irony, the churches themselves are among the principal agencies of secularization in America.

Many people come to church because they have at least a vague desire to find deeper meaning in life and at least a vague sense of the reality of the supernatural. The average person, no matter how deeply immersed in the secularity of daily life, seems to have no particular trouble believing in miracles, for example. If anything, it could be argued that Americans of the past decade have been too credulous about all sorts of supernatural claims. Church leaders, however, often function in such a way as to dampen religious fervor and undermine religious belief. Unless they choose carefully, people who join a church may find themselves less religious than before. From the pulpit, in religious education classes, and in the religious press they may find themselves ceaselessly propagandized in the direction of secularist views of personal morality, politics, and a host of other things. They are continually pressed to understand the "true meaning" of their faith in essentially secular ways.

The reasons for this strange state of affairs are complex. Briefly, they arise from the fact that for a long time, in most denominations, the education of clergy and other church leaders has been carried on in seminaries which look primarily to the secular intellectual world for their authority. Not uncommonly, seminary professors are more respectful of the reigning authorities in psychology, philosophy, or sociology than they are of the authority of the church itself. It is perhaps in the seminaries where the habit of always glancing over one's shoulder at Christianity's "cultured despisers" is most deeply ingrained.

Such attitudes perpetuate themselves throughout most denominations—at official conferences, in official publications, in national and regional offices. For the most part denominational posts are filled by people who have accepted a secularized Christianity almost completely, who feel uneasy in the presence of more conservative church members, and who feel it their duty to win over the "backward" to newer points of view. These "advanced" cadres of the church are often extremely skillful in using the levers of power in each denomination. They perpetuate themselves, or people like themselves, in key positions, and give, at best, token recognition to the orthodox.

Yet although the secularizers have gotten control of perhaps a majority of American denominations, the future probably does not lie with them. Since the 1960s, membership in the more liberal churches has been declining, while membership in the conservative churches has been growing, in some cases rather dramatically.

There is no finer irony than this, that the people who have been so sure that they were making Christianity "relevant" to the modern world turn out to be those who are losing followers, while the supposedly outmoded denominations are attracting them. The explanation is not mysterious. The world is indeed becoming more secular, as the liberals recognize. But, precisely because of that secularity, religion of all kinds, including liberal religion, has a diminishing appeal. Many Americans have now become so secularized that they cannot see the point of any church, liberal or not. The liberal churches are losing members both because they have driven away many of their more orthodox supporters and because they have "liberated" their parishioners from traditional religion to the extent that these people see no need for religion of any kind.

The more conservative churches are growing, however, because there is an apparent hunger for religion after the determined secularity of the past twenty years. This is evident especially among the young. There are sizable groups of orthodox young people even on college campuses, something that would have been almost unthinkable even as late as 1975. Many people now realize that valuable things were thrown away heedlessly in the midst of the frenetic rebelliousness of the period 1965-75. They are now looking to rediscover what they lost and are coming to realize that the liberal churches cannot provide guidance.

There is yet another way in which the future of Christianity probably belongs to the orthodox. The process of secularization in the liberal churches is almost inexorable. At this point it could not be reversed even if its leaders wanted to reverse it, which they do not. (At most, they slow the process when they fear they are alienating too many people.) The next logical step, which has already been urged by some, is to abandon all claims to being Christian, on the grounds that Christianity is too narrow and confining a designation. God has, according to the avant-garde view, revealed himself equally in all the cultures of the world. There is no justification for positing the uniqueness, much less the superiority, of Christianity. ("God" is in any case merely a metaphor for whatever man finds "ultimate" in life.)

By the end of this century, many of the liberal churches will no longer call themselves Christian and will make no special effort to keep alive Christian traditions in doctrine, worship, or ethics. Local churches will have allowed themselves to be transformed into all-purpose community centers in which many kinds of presumably beneficial activities go on but in which no special religious claims are made.

Thus, as the third millenium of the Christian era begins, Christians will be fewer in number than they are now, but it will be a precious designation because claimed only by those who truly believe in Christ's name.

NINE

True and False Humanism

THE TERM "HUMANISM" is ambiguous from a Christian stand-point. In one sense its common use is to be welcomed, since it tends to make things clear. Christians ultimately trust in God, Humanists in themselves. In another sense, it is unfortunate that religious believers have allowed nonbelievers to preempt the term for their own use. In the end, Christians are the true humanists.

Secular Humanism rests on an unperceived fallacy. In effect it says that man can love and esteem himself more if he does not have to share that love and esteem with God. But love is something which grows the more it is shared. When men love God, their genuine self-love does not diminish, it increases. Finally, it is only because they love God that men are properly enabled to love themselves.

There is a long tradition in Christianity which warns against self-love. What is meant by that term is something fairly close to Secular Humanism—if not an outright atheism, then at least so close an attachment to one's own will that the will of God can have no place in one's life. Self-love in this sense is not love at all but a kind of narcissistic self-worship.

Modern liberal Christians are right in insisting that those who would love God must first love themselves in the true sense. It is something which orthodox Christians can forget, if they understand warnings against self-love in the wrong way or if they dwell on their sins to the exclusion of everything else about themselves. Where liberals go wrong is in often confusing genuine love of self with the narcissistic self-indulgence that spiritual teachers have always warned against.

Man must love himself because he is lovable in the sight of God. He is created in God's image and likeness and placed over God's creation. He is given talents which God expects to be used for his own glory, and to fulfill the divine plan. Although prone to sin, he is never rejected by God, until such time as the sinner in effect damns himself by his recalcitrance. Unrepentant sinfulness can often be a result of despair—the inability to believe that God could actually love or forgive the sinner. There are few things more open to misunderstanding, sometimes fatal misunderstanding, than Christian self-love. At the present time, it has been so distorted that it might seem better not to speak of it at all, but Christians cannot surrender love of humanity to nonbelievers.

The same is true with respect to the ambition to achieve a good society. There is no necessary opposition between belief in eternity and the will to make a better life on earth. The teachings of Christ have much to say about the responsibilities of men towards one another. The error is in a socialized form of perverted self-love, the belief that a good life on earth is all that matters and that men somehow "deserve" such a life. In modern times, it has been principally the secularists who have proposed a contradiction between time and eternity. Christians have been found in virtually every movement to transform the world. Unfortunately, many Christians have accepted the secularist assumption. They think they must prescind from all considerations of eternity so as not to distract themselves from the struggle for a better world.

Like self-love, the idea of the good society, which can be found in Christian thought going back to early centuries, is subject to crippling distortions. Perhaps the most lethal is the assumption that men somehow "deserve" earthly happiness in all its fullness. Christianity, drawing on the full range of human experience as well as on divine revelation, points out that the struggle for happiness is precisely that, a struggle. It is a struggle which will only be completed in God. On earth, because of sin and because of God's mysterious Providence, there will be many disappointments. The person who expects full earthly happiness as his birthright will inevitably fall into disappointment and bitterness. His last state will be worse than his first.

The ultimate failure of Secular Humanism is in the fact that of its very nature it promises what it cannot fulfill. By encouraging people to put their trust in earthly happiness it programs them for disillusionment. This is in large measure the reason why the history of the modern world has been characterized, intellectually, by philosophies of pessimism like Existentialism and by often-rancorous bitterness over various plans for worldly improvement. In the twentieth century, mass slaughter has been perpetrated not by religious believers in opposition to heresy but by secularists convinced that their plan for a worldly utopia is the only possible one.

It is not often noticed how modern totalitarianism is inherent in certain kinds of Secular Humanism. Totalitarianism is a political system which seeks to shape and control every aspect of people's lives in the interest of creating a perfect worldly society. Obviously, if one believes such a thing is possible, there is almost an obligation to try to bring it into being. Human happiness depends on it.

But people seem blind and shortsighted. Many resist conformity to the laws which promise to make them truly happy. They fail to obey blindly the nation-state and thus struggle against Fascism. They shortsightedly cling to their property and thus resist Communism. They persist in believing in God, which the prophets of the new age have identified as an obstacle to progress. They must therefore be forced to obey, because such obedience is in their own interest and that of humanity. In modern times much greater suffering has been perpetrated in the name of humanity than has ever been done in the name of religion.

Nor is this totalitarianism merely an unfortunate corruption of high-minded idealism. Karl Marx had already justified totalitarian methods in his writings, even as he justified violent revolution in the name of the working class. Religion in the modern world has been the strongest and most tenacious bulwark against totalitarianism. It claims individual obedience to a higher law and loyalty to a higher ruler, which makes impossible a blind obedience to earthly governments. Totalitarian governments are anti-religious on principle. They realize quite clearly that religion gives to each person, as it were, a zone of privacy and personal freedom. The religious believer can, if nothing else, be truly free in an inward sense, which the omnicompetent state cannot permit.

However, it would be unfair to judge Secular Humanism primarily on the basis of totalitarian states, such as Communist Russia. All genuine Communists are by definition Secular Humanists, since they deny God and place their faith in man. But most Secular Humanists are not Communists. They may, in fact, oppose Communism because of its denial of human freedom. (A good example is the Humanist philosopher Sidney Hook, who for most of his life has been equally resolute in both his anti-Communism and his anti-religious positions.)

There are, however, more benign forms of totalitarianism which are often not recognized as such. Many Humanists (and some religious believers) have become so exercised over the prospect of the over-population of the world, for example, that they now talk about enforced restrictions on human breeding. At a minimum this would involve incentives for people who do not have children and penalties for those who do. In a graduated process, it would end quite possibly with enforced abortions or enforced sterilizations for those who have "too many" children. Such methods have already been employed in China. Some Westerners who are not Communists nonetheless express admiration for the Chinese solution. Although Humanists are usually quite vigilant against anything they construe as a threat to individual liberty, they have been strangely silent about this prospect, when they not have actively endorsed it.

Another plausible door to what might be called "soft totalitarianism" is the concept of "mental health." The Soviet Union is known to use psychiatry as a means of silencing

Karl Marx (1818-83) was the most influential social thinker of modern times, the father of Communism, and the inspirer of many people who employ his ideas even if they stop short of making a full commitment to them. Marx condemned all religion utterly, not only because he claimed the churches were parties to an "oppressive" social order but, more importantly, because he thought religious belief distracted men from the earthly struggle in which they should be engaged. Typical was his opinion that "man, who in his search for a supernatural being in the fantasy reality of heaven found only a reflection of himself, will no longer be inclined to find only the semblance of his own self, a non-human being, when he seeks and must seek his true reality."

political dissidents or other inconvenient people. This practice has elicited strong protests from the West. However, such flagrant practices are not the only abuses of the concept of mental health. Implicit in much Humanistic Psychology, for example, is the assumption that people of strongly orthodox religious beliefs or firm moral principles are psychologically unhealthy. Such beliefs are treated as signs of a "rigid" and neurotic personality. So far, there have only been isolated instances of the power of law used against people deemed overly "fanatical" in their beliefs. (Religious beliefs have been used as a negative factor in deciding child-custody cases.)

The public mood of the 1980s, which is seen as in reaction to the excesses of the previous two decades, probably does not favor the extension of such practices. However, there is no doubt that some people in the "helping professions," with some political support, would gradually extend the power of the courts and other public agencies in such a way as to impose disabilities on people whose personal religious and moral beliefs are deemed unbalanced. This would include not only obvious and justified instances, such as cults which seem to brainwash their members, but people whose only offense is that they believe in things (the literal truth of the Bible, for example) in which no "rational" person could believe.

The battle over morality in the schools—sex education, values clarification, etc.—is actually an early round in this struggle. In effect, those who control the schools say that they have a right to "correct" the beliefs which students have learned at home or in church. There is a long-range tendency for the state to take more and more responsibility for the formation of children. This process many people would now extend to the level of comprehensive day-care centers beginning soon after infancy. Ideally, almost the whole responsibility for education of children should be taken out of the hands of parents who may inculcate their own "narrow" beliefs in their children.

Not all Humanists support this prospect, and some oppose it. On the whole, however, outspoken Humanists tend to be ranged on the side of those who might be called social engineers.

Their emphasis on personal freedom mainly serves to "liberate" people from traditional kinds of moral authority, especially family and church. Seldom do they extend the same freedom to those who want to be liberated from the authority of secularized schools though. Implicit in the Humanist perspective is the claimed ability to identify what is "best" for humanity and then to implement it through public policy. Thus, with few exceptions, Humanists support the inexorable growth of public agencies with more and more intrusive influence in people's private lives.

By denying man any link to eternity or any ability to transcend time, Humanists place man in bondage to history. The most extreme statement of this was made by Karl Marx, who made the march of history inexorable and prescribed for his followers a program of identifying and then supporting that march. Those who do not will, inevitably, be crushed by impersonal forces beyond any power of individual control. Marxism has derived much of its appeal from its claim to be in touch with the forces of change and its guarantee that its followers will end up on the victorious side in all historical conflicts.

However, all forms of Humanism, in effect, preach bondage to history, even if not as explicitly or systematically as Marxism. Most Humanists would allow man at least a measure of freedom and thus some ability to influence his destiny. But since man cannot transcend history, Humanism implies that he must make his peace with it. He is effectively passive before all the more "progressive" movements which history spawns. (There is much attachment, in liberal Humanist circles, to the notion of "an idea whose time has come." One by one the beliefs of the past must be systematically negated in order to make progress possible.)

It may appear that there is a contradiction here, since Humanist rhetoric concentrates so heavily on the notion of "freedom" and Humanists are so often ranged on the side of those seeking to "liberate" themselves from situations they consider oppressive. However, this espousal of freedom takes place within a narrow context only. It is mainly liberation from traditional kinds of moral authority and, increasingly, from personal moral responsibility, such as towards one's family. The result of this "liberation" is the creation of the atomized individual, the man who is "free" of all entanglements with family, church, religion, nation, etc., and who therefore stands isolated. Such individuals are wholly the prey of powerful forces which promise a better future and which are prepared to bring that future into being by coercion. The ideal Humanist "free" man is one who has thrown over the traces of past authorities but who, as a result, has made himself all the more malleable to future authorities. The atomized man thus produced is the raw material of totalitarianism, since he lacks the personal convictions or the social ties (family or religion) which would impel him to resist. When totalitarianism promises a future in which all the individual's "needs" are catered to, its promise becomes nearly irresistible.

Put another way, the prevailing Humanist idea of freedom tends to undermine the sense of personal moral responsibility which the individual possesses. It discredits the sources of this responsibility and systematically encourages people to assert their "rights" against all the demands of duty. (Thus if a parent abandons the family, it is assumed that this is because the parent's "need" outweighs whatever responsibility he or she owes the family.) No society can exist in a chaotic state in which personal moral responsibility is being systematically undermined. Thus, for the sake of order, people must be compelled to behave by superior force. Law rests no longer on a sense of moral rightness but on the demands of social order. The state must become more and more dictatorial simply as a way of insuring orderly behavior.

This is not to say that all Humanists are personally irresponsible. Many are good people trying to live moral lives. But most of this morality is the residue of thousands of years of religiously based ethics, an ethics which has been deeply ingrained in people all over the world. Humanists have not found a persuasive basis for morality which can command widespread acceptance. Nor have they discovered any effective means of inculcating moral belief in young people. Their attempts at moral education, as in the public schools, usually have the effect of discrediting whatever moral beliefs children already have.

One by one, basic principles of traditional morality are crumbling. This is most dramatic with regard to sexual behavior, but more ominous in the sanctity of human life. Avant-garde thinkers now routinely justify abortion, infanticide, and euthanasia. It seems clear that almost all moral "taboos" are under systematic assault. Although some Humanists may have misgivings about this, most support it at least passively, as part of man's continuing march towards progress and as further blows struck on behalf of personal freedom. Humanists have found no basis for a common human morality and do not seem particularly concerned about the problem.

Perhaps the greatest irony of Humanism is the fact that, in the end, it can no longer support the human freedom and dignity which it extols. This is graphically demonstrated in the appearance of B.F. Skinner's name on the second *Humanist Manifesto*. Skinner has written a book called *Beyond Freedom and Dignity*. He is perhaps America's most influential exponent of Behavioristic Psychology, which regards human actions as essentially the results of impersonal psychological stimuli rather than of free and reasoned decisions. Humanistic Psychology, for all its flaws, is infinitely preferrable to Behaviorism, in which man is reduced not only to a mere biological creature but almost to a mechanical automaton. Strangely, although not all Humanists are Behaviorists, they seem impervious to Behaviorism's assaults on humanity.

Another curious example of Humanism's eventual sapping of the foundations of human dignity is pornography. Not all Humanists defend pornography. Some no doubt find it offensive. But Humanists almost always defend the legal rights of pornographers. They have made the "right" to distribute pornography, almost without restriction, one of the key tests of the freedom of the press. Inevitably, however, many Humanists go beyond merely defending the legal rights of pornographers to defending the thing itself. This is certainly the case with Sol Gordon, also a signer of the second *Humanist Manifesto,* whose work in sex education has tended towards abolishing any distinction between pornography and healthy sex. *The Humanist* magazine, although admitting to some misgivings about pornography, nonetheless, on the whole, defends it.

This is ironic because pornography is surely one of the greatest anti-human manifestations of contemporary culture. Pornographic literature and films have advanced far beyond pictures of undressed women or descriptions of sex acts to sado-masochism and every other kind of perversion. Contemporary pornography appeals to the desire to debase, punish, even to annihilate the human body. It is strange that it is defended by those who claim to be promoting a "healthy" attitude towards sex.

Humanists (and some misguided Christians) mainly defend pornography because they have accepted the human ego as the ultimate criterion of moral rightness. Thus, although they may have personal misgivings about it, they cannot bring themselves to condemn it. That would be interference with freedom. To state unequivocally that pornography is bad would be to invoke some objective moral standard higher than the individual, which Humanists find unacceptable.

In addition, many Humanists take satisfaction from all acts of what might be called moral transgression. Every time an individual defies some traditional moral rule this is seen as an admirable expression of freedom which expands the limits of human behavior. As such it is to be welcomed, even if one has reservations about the act itself. Here, as elsewhere, Humanists try to draw a line at the point where defiant moral acts begin to "hurt someone." In contemporary pornography there are many ways in which people are deliberately hurt, including in some cases the actual killing of human victims for the titillation of the spectator. While Humanists disapprove of this, they do not recognize that it is the logical outcome of the pornographic

B.F. Skinner is the chief representative of the psychological school called Behaviorism, which dominates a good part of the psychological world in America. Behaviorism is not only irreligious; it is also anti-humanistic, in that it treats human beings almost like delicate machines, operated by various kinds of controls. Behaviorists, like some other people enamored of science, refuse to believe in the reality of anything which cannot be verified by laboratory investigation. Skinner's best-known book has the significant title *Beyond Freedom and Dignity*.

mind which they justify. In practice they tend to leave it to each individual as to whether his actions "hurt" others.

The great seventeenth-century Christian apologist Blaise Pascal wrote, "He who plays the angel plays the beast." When man aspires to a higher place in creation than the one to which he is entitled, he ends up in a lower place. Contemporary Humanists do not play the angel in the obvious sense of comparing themselves to angels. They do not believe in a spiritual world. They do aspire to be angelic in the sense that they regard man as the pinnacle of the universe, the highest level of existence, able to dispense with God. They also free man from any necessary obedience to an objective moral law, confident that if given complete freedom man will eventually learn to live responsibly and virtuously.

Contemporary society shows in many ways how mistaken that belief is. As man more and more declares his independence from traditional moral and religious constraints he does not soar to the heights of Nietzsche's superman, but finds himself more and more drawn down by his lower nature. He can no longer even distinguish between his higher and lower natures but feels compelled to rationalize whatever it is that human beings actually do. Popular culture over the past twenty years has exhorted men to exalt themselves, cater to themselves, almost to adore themselves. Yet the result has been that people have sunk deeper and deeper into moral and spiritual confusion and social breakdown. The formulas proclaimed to exalt men and make them happy have led to debasement and cynicism.

As the Jesuit theologian Henri DeLubac showed in his book, *The Drama of Atheist Humanism* (primarily a study of nineteenth-century atheism), every Humanist system in the end betrays man. There is a major and inevitable gulf between what it promises and what it is able to fulfill.

Humanism promises total freedom, but man can exercise freedom, paradoxically, only in fulfillment of the commands of his Creator. All men chafe against the limitations of life, but the Humanist acts of defiance and heedless disregard end by enslaving the individual to his passions and to the inexorable march of history.

Since man was created by an all-wise and all-loving God, he cannot be truly free or truly happy except in loving obedience to his Creator's will. "You shall know the truth, and the truth shall make you free."

Notes

Chapter One
What Is Secular Humanism?

1. *Humanist Manifestoes I and II* (Buffalo, N.Y.: Prometheus Books, 1973), pp. 7-11.
2. *Ibid.*, pp. 13-31.
3. Paul Kurtz, ed., *The Humanist Alternative* (Buffalo, N.Y.: Prometheus Books, 1975), p. 177.

Chapter Seven
The Law and the Constitution

1. The subject is most thoroughly discussed in Frank Sorauf, *The Wall of Separation: The Constitutional Politics of Church and State* (Minneapolis: University of Minnesota Press, 1976).
2. Pfeffer, "The 'Catholic' Catholic Problem," *Commonweal*, Aug. 1, 1975, pp. 302-303, and "Issues That Divide: The Triumph of Secular Humanism," *Journal of Church and State*, 1977, pp. 203-205.
3. See, for example, Douglas book, *The Bible and the Public Schools* (Boston: Little Brown, 1966).
4. Hugo Black, Jr., *My Father Hugo Black* (New York: Random House, 1975.)

Chapter Eight
The Secularization of the Churches

1. *Humanist Manifesto I*, pp. 9-10.
2. Kurtz, ed., *The Humanist Alternative*, p. 185.

Index